EUCHARIST

Toward the Third Millennium

EUCHARIST
Toward the Third Millennium

GERARD AUSTIN

MARY COLLINS

STEPHEN HAPPEL

KEVIN W. IRWIN

MARGARET MARY KELLEHER

FREDERICK R. McMANUS

DAVID N. POWER

GERARD SLOYAN

LTP

LITURGY
TRAINING
PUBLICATIONS

Acknowledgments

This book was edited by Martin F. Connell. Deborah Bogaert was the production editor, with assistance from Theresa Houston. Barb Rohm designed the book, and Jim Mellody-Pizzato was the production artist who set the type in New Baskerville and Syntax. Printed by Versa Press, Inc. of East Peoria, Illinois.

Cover art is by Jean Troxel.

Eucharist : toward the third millennium / Gerard Austin . . . [et al.].

      p. cm.

    Papers presented at a symposium held to celebrate the 25th anniversary liturgy program at Catholic University.

    Includes bibliographical references.

    1. Lord's Supper—Catholic Church—Congresses. I. Austin, Gerard.

BX2215.2.E88   1997

264'.02—dc21   97-9976

                                             CIP

ISBN 1-56854-181-3

V2EUCH

Table of **Contents**

Introduction

KEVIN W. IRWIN

It began quite simply. A colleague, Kate Dooley, offered a written suggestion for the liturgical studies faculty agenda: "Are we going to do anything to mark the twenty-fifth anniversary of the program?" For those of us not among the founding fathers and mothers, it came as a surprise that Catholic University's liturgy program was that old. But in fact, as a result of the clear directives of the Constitution on the Sacred Liturgy of Vatican II (15 – 18), the program was established a quarter-century ago. In the early days, Fred McManus, still very much involved in implementing the Constitution internationally, was ably assisted by the recently doctored professors Gerard Austin and R. Kevin Seasoltz. Their respective expertise in liturgical law, liturgical sources, and symbol, myth and ritual were reflected in the first courses taught in the new program. Today the faculty boasts eight full-time professors — the largest year-round liturgy faculty in the United States.

The faculty unanimously agreed that we should indeed do something to mark the program's anniversary. As our discussions ensued, it was clear that we wanted not to tell our history but to aid our alumni, alumnae and colleagues to move toward ever new vistas in implementing the liturgical renewal of Vatican II — especially as we looked toward the approach of the new millennium. In the years between the founding of the program and today, the method of liturgical study itself has developed and matured. We wanted to demonstrate this and to move the discussion forward even more.

The choice of the eucharist as our focus came easily. From conversations with our students and with colleagues nationwide, as well as from our own involvement in dioceses and parishes, it was clear that a new "moment" had come for the eucharist both academically and pastorally. Some of the issues that had recently surfaced were quite new: what to do, for example, about Sunday worship in the absence of a priest. Other questions were given new urgency or a new focus: the role of women in the liturgical assembly and music for the eucharistic prayer. Some questions called for new definition and shape: the meaning of a liturgical theology of the eucharist and the adequacy of liturgical preaching. Some questions concerned the shape and scope of liturgical studies itself: specifically, an interdisciplinary approach that included ritual studies and inculturation. It was agreed that there was more than ample material on the eucharist as we looked to the year 2000 and beyond.

In structuring the symposium, we wanted to bridge the often separate worlds of the academic and the pastoral. We did this by inviting contributions from a number of our faculty, whose presentations would lead to questions and answers and a large-group, structured dialogue. The papers printed here are thus of a specific genre. They were intended to be focused, fairly brief (20 minutes each) and aimed to support dialogue with the symposium participants.

Because of his recently published and highly acclaimed book *The Eucharistic Mystery*,[1] David Power was the logical choice to begin the presentations. Through "A Prophetic Eucharist in a Prophetic Church" he offered a characteristically insight-filled and compelling presentation on the eucharist as the church approaches new cultural, sociological and theological arenas as well as "the third millennium" itself. Issues of church order and the centrality of the eucharist were approached judiciously, yet prophetically, with wise analysis and concrete challenges.

In line with her clear interest in broadening liturgical method to include the actual performance of the rites,[2] Margaret Mary Kelleher's paper "Ritual Studies and the Eucharist: Paying Attention to Performance" offered a clear summary of how the work of ritual theorists can contribute significantly to how we interpret what the eucharist is by interpreting what the church does when it celebrates the eucharist.

In light of my own methodological interest in liturgical theology,[3] it was agreed that I should address "The Critical Task of Liturgical Theology." This meant reflecting on the adequacy of the present rite of the eucharistic liturgy in light of the historical evolution and theological meaning of the liturgy itself. At the same time, I wanted to indicate that the celebration of the eucharist challenges some assumptions of contemporary American society. The demise of regular patterns of family dining in fact diminishes Catholic notions of sacramentality and the way we experience Christ's presence in table companionship.

Gerard Austin's paper, *"In Persona Christi* at the Eucharist," reflects and follows up on some of David Power's insights and demonstrates how he himself has moved from previous publications about liturgical sources, confirmation and Sunday worship in the absence of a priest.[4] In this paper he considers the issue of who celebrates the eucharist and the meaning of the traditional and recently revived term *in persona Christi*. His articulation of some of the most theologically and liturgically significant theories indicates that this whole area is a "work in progress" in liturgical studies today.

From as far back as her important commentary on the theology and practice of the communion rite[5] through her most recent essays on the theology and practice of liturgy,[6] one of Mary Collins's methodological themes has concerned how to support what liturgy is theoretically intended to do — to be a communal celebration of the church's self-awareness and identity in Christ. Her paper, "Liturgical Homily: Connecting the Body," continues this theme from her writings by asserting a theology of ecclesial preaching, critiquing some conventional preaching practices and offering suggestions for achieving greater unity of the whole body of Christ as it celebrates the eucharist.

After a break for lunch, informal conversations and perhaps a walk around campus, we reconvened for the afternoon sessions. Again the emphasis was on discussion with the presenters — one faculty member and the rest alumni and alumnae of our program. The single contribution included here is from the program's "founder," Fred McManus. In "Pastoral Ecumenism: The Common Lectionary" he articulates both the theory and practice of ongoing efforts toward establishing a common lectionary cycle of readings. Written with characteristic clarity and logic, this paper offers an important example of the nature of Vatican II's liturgical reform — that is, ongoing and meant to develop beyond an *editio typica* to ritual books that are necessarily adapted to the needs of local churches. It also gives a much-needed emphasis on how *lex orandi, lex credendi* should include the word proclaimed and preached at liturgy and not just euchological texts and liturgical symbols.

The other afternoon sessions included presentations and discussions on relating liturgical theology and ecclesiology to suitable worship spaces for the eucharist (John Buscemi), priestless Sundays (James Dallen),[7] how to interpret the increasing demand for eucharistic devotions and how to implement eucharistic devotion outside of Mass appropriately (Joseph

Fortuna), and a pastoral approach to the question of the formative nature of the liturgy (Gabe Huck). In addition, there were especially lively discussions about the adequacy of some contemporary settings for the sung eucharistic prayer, some of which were sung at the session (Richard Fragomeni), about the question of women in the liturgical assembly (Catherine Vincie), and about the emerging area of liturgical inculturation, particularly in terms of gesture and dance (Thomas Kane). Clearly, each of these topics reflected the focus of the symposium — to help move toward the future of eucharistic celebration in our church equipped with insights from our theological and liturgical tradition.

At the same time that we wanted to bridge the academic and pastoral sides of church life, we also wanted the symposium to reflect the resources of Catholic University and the way that other departments of the university could contribute to an integral and integrated study of liturgy. Largely through the efforts of Stephen Happel (Chair of the Department of Religion and Religious Education), Roland Reed of the university's drama department agreed to produce and direct a performance of the medieval mystery play *Covenants*. As the description of this liturgical/theatrical event by Dr. Happel contained here indicates, it was an astounding and moving experience for all of us.

The play's theme has as much pertinence today as it did when it was written in the fifteenth century. The play retells God's gracious covenant initiative in saving history, from Adam and Eve and their expulsion from Eden, through Cain's murder of Abel, to Noah's escape from the great flood, to the sacrifice of Isaac. The active participation of the assembly by singing at various times both solidified its meaning for us and indicated how the notions of involvement in such dramas and in the liturgy itself are all parts of a piece.

The symposium began with this miracle play; it ended with the celebration of the eucharist. Both took place at Saint Vincent's Chapel on the university campus. The final scene of *Covenants* concerned the dramatic reenactment of Abraham's sacrifice of Isaac, at the very altar where, 24 hours later, we would celebrate the eucharistic renewal of the new covenant in Jesus. The homily delivered at the closing eucharist—with which this collection of papers concludes—was truly fitting. Preached by Gerald Sloyan, who also led us in the eucharist that night, the homily speaks compellingly and prophetically about the value of what we were about at the symposium and what we are about more broadly in liturgical renewal. The themes of the play *Covenants* were not new to any of us, but because of its compelling rhetoric, music and drama, that production enabled us to come to appreciate them as if for the first time. As Abraham was about to slay his only son, not a word or sound was heard. We were all caught up in this reenacted act of faith. The symposium ended in the same way. We were keenly attuned to the music we sang, the gestures and movement of the liturgical action we engaged in, and the words of Father Sloyan in the homily and in the sung eucharistic prayer commemorating and narrating the "new and everlasting covenant" as well as the "mystery of faith" of the eucharist.

Endnotes

1. New York: Crossroad, 1992.

2. See "Hermeneutics in the Study of Liturgical Performance," *Worship* 67 (July 1993): 292–318; and "Liturgical Theology: A Task and a Method," *Worship* 67 (January 1988): 2–25.

3. See *Context and Text: Method in Liturgical Theology* (Collegeville: The Liturgical Press, 1994).

4. See Gerard Austin, *Anointing with the Spirit* (New York: Pueblo, 1985); and "Communion Services: A Break with Tradition," in *Fountain of Life,* ed. Gerard Austin (Washington: Pastoral Press, 1991), pp. 199–215.

5. See "Historical Perspectives," in *It's Your Own Mystery* (Washington: The Liturgical Conference, 1977), pp. 7–15.

6. See "Eucharist and Christology Revisited: The Body of Christ," *Theology Digest* 39:4 (Winter 1992): 321–32.

7. See *The Dilemma of Priestless Sundays* (Chicago: Liturgy Training Publications, 1994).

The Interaction of Two Genres
Roland Reed's *Covenants* and the Drama of the Eucharist

STEPHEN HAPPEL

Our tragic author [the presider] represents by his gestures in the theater of the church before the Christian people the struggle of Christ, and teaches them the victory of his redemption" (Honorius of Autun, Gemma Animae, ca. 1100).

Isaac, a youthful, thin fellow in a T-shirt and khakis, sits cross-legged, bound and blindfolded upon the eucharistic table above a stone embedded with martyrs' bones. He winces with pain as his father Abraham sweeps a bright, stainless, new butcher's knife before his unseeing eyes. "Is it God's will you kill me with your knife? . . . Then you must do what God has bid. But tell not my mother what you did."[1]

Abraham delays; he cannot bear the sound of his son's voice. So the victim must become the agent:

> Seeing I must needs be dead,
> Of one thing I will you pray,
> Since I must die the death today,
> As few strokes take as well you may
> When you smite off my head.

Abraham, vulnerable only to the voice of God, cries out: "Now my dear son, here shalt thou lie, /Unto my work now must I hie; /I had as lief myself to die." Chanting Kaddish, Abraham raises his knife. At the climactic moment, the audience gulps in the silent vacuum. In the gap, God announces:

> Abraham, thou art spared to sacrifice thy son today,
> But know that, free of sin, one day,
> For to win all mankind's grace
> My own lad will be taken to a place
> Of sacrifice, and for all men good and ill,
> Will be done to death upon a hill.

A butchers' dance would celebrate the divine intervention, the freeing of Isaac and the reunion of this family; but the final ritual could not heal the psychic incision that made absolutely clear the bloody cost of human reconciliation with God.

The story of Abraham's test concluded a polarizing history of divine inventiveness and Lucifer's pride, Adam and Eve's betrayal of each other, Cain's cursed wandering after his murder of Abel and Noah's inability to meet his wife as an equal except during perilous storms and floods. Conflict and anger, alienation and fear, death and despair—the legacy of an original struggle between love and malice at the heart of the universe. Can there be anything else?

Covenants: The Mystery Play

The production of *Covenants* at Saint Vincent's Chapel opened the celebration of the twenty-fifth anniversary of the liturgical studies program in the School of Religious Studies at Catholic University of America.[2] *Covenants* was the first half of a cycle of medieval mystery plays adapted by Roland Reed of the university's drama department. The symposium concluded with an anticipatory eucharist for Sunday, the following day. The same altar on which Isaac was sacrificed became the table for the breaking of bread in the *anamnesis* of Christ's death and resurrection.

page 3

 Covenants has reworked in a contemporary idiom the major themes in the history of redemption found in the English mystery plays. These 500-year-old dramas articulate a give-and-take in divine-human affairs that narrates both a rather deadly game and a macabre comedy routine. Once God becomes a character portrayed by actors *within* a narrative, divine omnipotence can show up as arbitrary and somewhat limited. Isaac's "don't tell my mother" marks a seemingly unilateral decision by a highly patriarchal divinity, replaced only by God's willingness to sacrifice the divine self for the sake of humanity. Nonetheless, having decided to create human beings as subjects who can genuinely return love, God binds the divine life to the freedom of women and men who hate one another and reject divine generosity.

 From the beginning, Lucifer seems compelled to compete with other creatures and with God. "For like a lord am I lifted by right to this light, /More fair than my peers and more might." In the play, God's hopes for the angelic choirs are destroyed by Lucifer's fantasies; so God creates humanity to "fulfill the bliss." Divine abundance requires a pleroma of finite beings to complete a continually expanding divine glory. It is as though God must colonize creation with love but at the same time permit, and even encourage, humanity's independence.

 Reed cast the play with working-class men and women who dressed in ordinary clothes. They took different roles, depending on the scene's needs, shifting characters with costumes and props. The earthy humor and strikingly concrete images of salvation were preserved from their medieval antecedents, while at the same time the use of modern implements constantly reminded the audience of the timeliness of the stories. In this production, Cain killed Abel with his tractor-wrench. The banter between Adam and Eve, Noah and his wife, and God and Abraham reflected the honest psychology of the medieval world. The audience was not surprised to hear and see Adam's naive confusion at the creation of an equal but different partner; nor were they amazed that Adam would make Eve the scapegoat for his own choices. The Serpent, the same actor who played Lucifer, was a streetwise dealer in easy solutions; but the domestic violence of Noah to his wife, and then hers to him in return, painfully escalated the human capacity for malice.

In these plays, salvation depicted a homely reality, buried within the quotidian dimensions of human life. The interventions of Transcendence were chronicled from inside the interactions of creation, making clear that the medium through which God saves the universe requires the cooperation of created reality. For example, Abel offered the best lamb from his flock; he told Cain that "God gives thee all thy living," that "all the good that thou has won, /Of God's grace alone is done." Cain, however, when he brought his wheat to the altar of sacrifice, complained that he did not have good wheat this year, only thistles and briars. He chose to be mean-spirited, ungenerous.

> ABEL: Cain, thou tythes wrong and of the worst,
> Ye should give God but best and first.

> CAIN: Not as much, great or small
> As he might wipe his arse withal.
> For that, all this that lies here
> Have cost me full dear;
> Ere it was shorn and brought in stack,
> Had I many a weary back.

Cain's sense of his life is that he has done the work; therefore, he should receive the reward. The continuing sense of the mystery play is that life and food, however meager, are gifts of love that can only be returned. Consistently, the scenes demonstrate that life is hard, but if human beings respond with bitterness, they have missed the point of the story. Learning how to respond with self-sacrifice is not masochism but authentic personal fulfillment.

page 5

The *thematic content* of these mystery plays mirrors the sacrificial message of the eucharist — the self-gift of God grants salvation to all human beings, and the only way to respond is by a similar gift of self. Divine love *requires* creation's cooperation for its efficacy.

The *form* of drama has something to teach us about the nature of the eucharist as well. Western European drama was reinvented, at least partially, through its emergence from the eucharistic liturgy. Since form and content cannot be divided in an absolute fashion, what can we learn about the eucharist from its generative relationship to drama? Here are two seemingly distinct genres (worship and theater), yet in their past they were intimately connected. It is also worth asking what sorts of connections are now being developed between these two forms of human expression.

In what follows, it will be necessary to outline some of the history through which the medieval genre of worship generated Western drama. This will situate some of the reasons for the use of Roland Reed's *Covenants* in a symposium on the eucharist. But the goal is more complex: What kind of dramatic elements are *now* operative in post–Vatican II worship? As a believing community, are we clear on how we want to develop those dramatic elements of worship? Do they reinforce or destroy the *thematic* contents of the eucharist? This final section will raise more questions about the future of eucharistic assemblies than it will answer, but the issues must be raised if our communities are to speak not just to themselves but to the world. What is the meaning of our eucharistic worship within a culture of such spectacles as grand theater and sports events, and of fast foods as a replacement for the family meal?

STEPHEN HAPPEL

Drama and Liturgy:
Two Genres Intertwined in History

The dialectic between public theater and Christian worship is complex historically and significant theoretically. Early Christians engaged in worship that was familial in style, focused on an extended family unit.[3] Eventually, the solemn, formal processions, chants and prayers of post – Constantinian worship in large basilica-shaped churches replaced pre – Christian drama, dance and mime in temples and public theaters. Christian antiquity's distaste for the frivolous pretense of comedic acting and the condemnation of violent and/or sexually explicit themes in plays and public displays marked the developing culture of the newly legitimated religion. Since dramas, stadium events, actors and gladiators were all related to the *demimonde* in antiquity, they were generally condemned.[4] There was a similar opposition to the public or private use of classical music.[5] Ancient Christian writers — like Cyprian, Novatian and Lactantius — believed, with their counterparts in Stoic philosophy, that the arousal of too much passion through music or drama was dangerous.

The rhetorical issue, however, was even more problematic, since elegant words could persuade to vice just as easily as to virtue. As Lactantius said:

> For the subject of comedies is the dishonoring of young
> girls, or the loves of harlots; and the more eloquent they
> are who have composed the accounts of these disgraceful
> actions, the more do they persuade by the elegance of
> their sentiments. . . . What can young men or young girls
> do when they see these things practiced without shame
> and willingly behold all? They are plainly admonished
> about what they can do, and are inflamed with lust, which
> is especially excited by seeing. . . . And they approve of
> these things while they laugh at them, and with vices

clinging to them, they return more corrupted to their apartments.[6]

Christian apologists joined this suspicion of seeing to the ideas of their Jewish forebears who argued that the use of visual images, especially any iconic representation of the divine, was illegitimate. The true image of God *(imago Dei)* was the human being, created and saved in Christ. This image was not aesthetic, but ethical; the virtuous lives of Christians were their best defense against the sporadic persecutions during late antiquity.[7]

page 7

In Egeria's account of her pilgrimage to the Holy Land during the fourth century, the woman from Galicia points to a liturgical origin for the dramatic reenactments during Holy Week. The pilgrims' way required movement in Jerusalem and the Holy Land from one stational church to another, motion that ultimately focused not only upon sacred places but upon sacred relics such as the true cross of Christ. The narratives of the gospel paralleled the passage of penitents and pilgrims as they travelled from one church to another, participating in the elaborate liturgical celebrations. There was a common desire to relive in spirit the events narrated by the evangelists.[8]

In the early medieval church, theologians such as Sophronius (560–638) in the East and Amalarius of Metz (780–850) in the West took the rubrics of public worship and turned them into dramas, either as a mimesis of the heavenly liturgy, in the East, or as a historicization of the life and death of Jesus, in the West.[9] Sophronius believed that the liturgy mediated symbolically the "life of Christ from the cradle to the grave."[10] The altar became the tomb, the preparation table was Calvary, and the stone ambos the doors to the tomb. The corporal was a burial shroud, while the ministers acted as the choirs of angels with their stoles the wings.[11] By the time of Amalarius of Metz in the West, the eucharistic elevation after the rite of institution had become a sign of raising Christ on the cross.[12] "The vicar of Christ does all these things in memory of the first advent of Christ. He kisses the altar to show the coming of Christ into Jerusalem."

Amalarius began to invent rubrics to make the liturgy more like the historical drama that it re-presented. The presider, the better to call to mind Christ's deeds, should ascend to the chair after having completed his labor of ministry in the *Gloria;*[13] after the *Gloria,* "Christ ascends into heaven to sit at the right hand of the Father." At the major elevation, Christ was being raised on the cross. At the *Nobis quoque peccatoribus,* the centurion has cried out that this was a just man, with the priest designating this narrative change through a loud shift in his voice. At the minor elevation, Joseph of Arimathea has taken down Jesus's body.

Christ had become the *real* or *actual* agent at the eucharist through the rubrical actions of the presider. One acts for the other. This, of course, confirmed and developed the continuing emphasis on the presider as the primary agent in the eucharistic celebration. The service itself was no longer about what the assembly *is* but about who Christ *was* for believers in the past, extending his action into the present through the acts and words of the clergy. Moreover, the mode of presence became insistently dramatic; a reinvention of Western theater offered the medium through which the assembly attached itself to the past salvific events of the Christ. Largely illiterate Christians watched while the clergy enacted the ritual drama.

Writers after Amalarius became even more schematic about history and ritual. For Bernold of Constance (ca. 1085), the canon was a most potent commemoration of the passion of Christ, acted out *(actitari)* according to the command of the Lord in the Gospel.[14] For the latter, the ritual gestures became a traditional way of making clear the *drama* of salvation. Honorius of Autun, from whose writings comes the epigraph that frames this article, explicitly locates the role of the presider as an actor—and an actor in the person of Christ.

At the same moment theologians were visually connecting rubrics and history, monastic communities were developing plays about personified virtues and virtuous saints, presenting them within the cloister, and writing passion plays for use at liturgy. Hrotswitha of Gandersheim produced six

dramatic pieces in Latin during the tenth century, hoping to provide "an edify-
ing version of Terence's immoral comedies."[15] Hildegard of Bingen, polymath
of her time, wrote morality plays for her community that pitted good virtues
against evil demons. The characters were highly realized allegorizations, and
they contained sophisticated emotional and psychological inwardness.

page 9

By the tenth century, however, representations of the *Quem Quaeritis*
responsory at Eastertime were acted *during* liturgy by three brothers clothed
in capes and holding censers, acting like those seeking the tomb. "They act
here in imitation of the angel sitting on the tombstone, and of the women
coming with their herbs to anoint the body of Jesus."[16]

The genesis of the liturgical drama can be found in the use of these
tropes, the verbal and musical amplifications of passages in the locally "standard" liturgical books. Sung elaborations of the *Kyrie, Agnus Dei* and responsory psalms first appeared in the eighth century in the West but flourished
in the tenth century, when they were given dramatic rubrics. The *Quem
Quaeritis* tropes were sung antiphonally before the Introit of the Easter morning eucharist. The oldest extant examples from the tenth century were trans-
ferred to the conclusion of Matins before the final *Te Deum*. Their remains
can be recognized in the dialogue between the angels and Mary in the current Easter Sunday sequence.

Eventually, the *Quem Quaeritis* tropes became a play, the *Visitatio
Sepulchri,* of which we have some 400 early versions. Plays on the passion of
Christ existed in Italy (Monte Cassino) from the twelfth century, in Germany
from the thirteenth and in France from the fourteenth, with the more com-
prehensive religious cycles of England (from which *Covenants* was compiled)
emerging during the late fourteenth century.

By the early eleventh century, monks began developing Christmas
tropes, then plays about the birth of Christ. In cathedrals and monastic
churches, new dramas appeared on Christmas night and on the morning
of January 6.[17] The Christmas dialogue featured an exchange between the
shepherds and unnamed people at the manger. Choirboys in France who

processed with the clergy to the high altar were dressed as shepherds during this dialogue throughout the High Middle Ages. French influence spread liturgical plays into Catalonia in the eleventh century and into Castile in the twelfth century as the Roman rite began to supplant the older Mozarabic liturgy around 1080. By the middle of the fourteenth century, minor clergy of Saint Paul's in London were presenting the "History of the Old Testament" at Christmas.[18] Also in the fourteenth century, the Latin text or mixed Latin-vernacular texts gradually ceded to complete vernacular plays. As Donovan points out, the "boundary line separating *dramatic liturgy* from *liturgical drama* was thus often very thin."[19] These plays lasted in some form in liturgical usage until well into the eighteenth century.

Geoffrey of Vinsauf, an Englishman of the thirteenth century studying in Paris, enunciated a general catechetical principle in his treatise on poetry and rhetoric that justified the use of theater in the work of worship. Memory, he insisted, should be fed moderately. "To remain between satiety and hunger is the wiser practice."[20] Memory "craves what is delightful, not what is boring. . . . Let [knowledge] feed the mind in such a way that it is offered as a delight, not a burden to it." Although there were occasional ecclesiastical opponents to the use of drama in worship, the restrictions clearly did not hinder the development of religious plays. Thomas Aquinas himself claimed that

> play is necessary for the interaction of human life. . . .
> The job of actors, which is directed to develop solace for
> human beings, is not illicit in itself, nor are they in the
> state of sin when they are engaged in moderate play. . . .
> [A] man who is without mirth not only is lacking in play-
> ful speech but is also burdensome to others, since he is
> deaf to the moderate mirth of others. Consequently they
> are vicious and are said to be boorish or rude.[21]

The delight in dramatic pleasure was a catechetical tool for drawing the believer into identification with the story of Christ, the saints and, indeed, the history of God's plan.

Opposition, however, to liturgical drama developed throughout the Middle Ages. The monastic culture that nurtured liturgical drama sometimes rejected it, since the penitential and ascetic discipline of Benedictine and then Cistercian communities forbade blatant displays of piety, individualism and the cultivation of bodily pleasure. Dissenters in England in the fourteenth century opposed the emphasis on "seeing" as the primary mode of popular participation, with a stress on inwardness and individual faith.[22]

page 11

In the North of England, the fourteenth-century cycles of Corpus Christi plays, from which Roland Reed's *Covenants* was adapted, exercised an orthodox influence against the encroaching heretical rejection of seeing.[23] In 1395, in response to the promulgation of the feast in honor of the eucharist, a tract states: "The service of Corpus Christi made by Friar Thomas is untrue and painted full of false miracles."[24] A *Treatise on Miracle Plays* by a group of dissenters argued against dramatic depictions of Christ's passion because they necessarily demeaned the actual event. "Then, since the miracles of Christ and of his saints were thus effectual, as our religion assures us, no man should use in jest and play the miracles and works that Christ so earnestly wrought for our salvation." It is God who works conversion of the heart, not the externals of a play that might provoke audiences to weep. Miracle plays, says the tract, are not about feeding our religious intelligence but about delighting our bodies!

The cycles of medieval mystery plays had a cultural, indeed sacramentally transformative, role to play. "Like the eucharistic host itself, late medieval drama attempted a far-reaching unification of the sacred and the secular, of Christ and the community of the faithful."[25] The emphasis on the actual presence of Christ in the eucharistic species and the preaching on the continuing operation of Christ's sacrifice in the liturgy were located within a plan of salvation that focused not only on human need for change but on an entire history of salvation that required both human and divine self-sacrifice. Without the sacrifice of God's only Begotten One and human participation in that event, God's plan would not have been fulfilled. The dramas emphasized the bodily, ordinary qualities of this salvation.[26] Human beings were not saved through educating the mind but through transforming the entire person into a gift to God.

page 12

This can be seen in the Cain and Abel sections of these plays, even in the revised production in Roland Reed's *Covenants*. Abel invites Cain to worship through a sacrifice of wheat and sheep. Cain opposes tithing but begrudgingly offers the least desirable portions as a substitute. Cain has better things to do than worship; he has dedicated himself to hard work. Medieval viewers would have heard this as an exaltation of the active over the contemplative life. Monks and friars are pray-ers who live from the gifts of others; merchants and peasants work hard for their living. In effect, however, Cain refuses to be a beggar before his brother or before God, asserting not just his need to work but his own superior strength to take care of himself. Abel's calm optimism and brotherly generosity are approved as a sign of his serene acceptance of divine generosity. This produces God's approval as well as an abundant fruitfulness for his work.[27] But Abel's agricultural sacrifice to God is given at the cost of his own life; witness in worship becomes the testimony of martyrdom.

The mystery plays emphasize the daily dimensions of faith. Although there are some theologically didactic dimensions within the plays (most notably in the *N-Town Cycle*), more often the performed narratives themselves demonstrate how the Body of Christ is the assembled body of believers at risk in the world. To be allied with Adam, Abel, Noah and Abraham requires more than just verbal testimony.[28] The audience's participation is invited, not by an authorial presence but by actors who address the audience. Noah asks the hen-pecked husbands in the audience to identify with him. The shepherds should appeal to poor laborers. Unfortunately, it is also possible to find oneself in Lucifer and the serpentine tempter during the Eden scene.

There, the character's appeal is by way of contrast; he may appear clever, but he is dangerous. In the symposium's production of *Covenants,* Lucifer was a young street tough, slick, inviting and weighed down with gold chains. Lucifer's fault is that he wants to be divine, but on his own terms—not through God's generosity.[29]

The genres of worship and drama were profoundly interconnected in the medieval world; without the *cooperation* of culture and religion in *both* worship and drama, there would have been no presence of the transcendent dimension to the world. The popular form of the dramas, therefore, publicly corroborated the content of the eucharistic liturgy and its emphasis on divine self-sacrifice. The vernacular modes of theater appreciated the incarnational elements operative in the central worship of the church. Underlying the ways in which the divine and human characters interact in *Covenants* is a theo-poetic assumption. Humans can be divinized by God through the most ordinary worldly events in which they live their lives and through their cooperation with one another. The drama itself, by its very form, proclaims the message.

This creates some problems, however. Some have argued that in the Middle Ages, popular piety, worship and drama were simply mirrored versions of one another—the first more allegorically symbolic, the second more narrative in structure. "Should the nave . . . and altar of the church be considered a stage, and its windows, statues, images and ornaments a 'setting'"?[30] The formal continuities were matched by the thematic similarities.[31] Later secular drama paralleled the eucharist's comedic elements: rebirth despite death, transitions from guilt to innocence, and developments from separation to communion. The shift from sadness to joy in the eucharistic story concludes with a genuine theophany within the sight of and on the tongue of the participant. Joy, however, is bought at the price of death.

By the end of the Middle Ages, dramas of salvation, such as *Covenants,* had evolved into relatively autonomous performances outside liturgical services; but the services themselves had also evolved into narrative dramas, paralleled by catechetical and theological arguments about the way in which Christ acted through the priest and the ways in which the ministers' gestures and words had become theatrical recitation. This past interwoven cultural world raises questions for our post–Vatican II worship: What is the relationship between current eucharistic worship and contemporary drama? In the Middle Ages, eucharistic drama was part of a spectrum of cultural expression that led from the altar to the sacrifice of Isaac performed on a wagon outside in the church square. How does contemporary eucharistic performance appear in its cultural setting?

page 14

Post – Vatican II Liturgy and Contemporary Drama: Demotic vs. Spectacular

Early-twentieth-century theologians could maintain that Catholic liturgical practice was not like secular drama. The differentiation of worship from public drama after the Middle Ages seemed clear and distinct. Not only were some nineteenth- and twentieth-century dramas explicitly antireligious, they also maintained their integrity as art for art's sake—an aesthetic artifact to be appreciated at a distance. This has now changed.

Contemporary dramatic performance has significantly shifted so that it is much closer to the kind of folk theater and liturgy that produced *Covenants,* with both its *spectacular* and *demotic* elements.[32] In this section, it will be necessary to provide some historical context for the role that current liturgical performance plays in Euro–American culture by briefly outlining recent developments in drama. This slight detour will permit us to see what choices the church now has with regard to worship forms in the late twentieth century. *Covenants* fell within a cultural spectrum that included worship. Within what cultural spectrum does Catholic eucharistic worship now fall?

Drama after the eighteenth-century Enlightenment has taken two paths: the thirst for a "naturalist realism" and the "idea play."[33] In all cases, neither gritty, dramatic realism nor the various forms of idea-play — absurdist, socialist, communist, existentialist and so forth — matched the aesthetic dimensions of Catholic eucharistic practice. Pre–Vatican II worship was in Latin; clergy wore stiff, ceremonial costumes; the actors were self-effacing and, at the same time, self-consciously hierarchical and hieratic. The attendant aesthetic dimensions of Gregorian chant, incense and formal movements belied comparison with "realist" dramas. In some ways, eucharistic celebrations probably bore more relationship to the rituals of Japanese Nō drama than to their Western artistic siblings. Even if in some Baroque churches the elaborate proscenium behind which the eucharist was performed framed a large cast of ritualizers, the traditional "fourth wall" (the audience) did not seem to be realized. The hallowed alienation of eucharistic liturgy from the patterns of ordinary life provided a difference that located it beyond the realm of drama. This was for many Catholics the "proper" *dramatic form* or network of metaphors for expressing transcendence.

page 15

In addition, liturgy was personally engaging and communicated with God. Post–Enlightenment drama did not "address" anyone, let alone the transcendent God; its language was not meant to provoke personal or community transformation. Interaction between one side of the proscenium and the other was limited to applause at the end of the performance. Only in this area did nineteenth- and twentieth-century Catholic worship offer parallel artistic performances; neither seemed to engage the audience directly except in "asides." Art was "for its own sake"; only as a byproduct might it edify the audience privately. All were to carry away their own personal meanings.

However, contemporary dramatic performance and theory have changed this "intellectual location" for drama. At once satire about the "normal" world, philosophical critique of ordinary rhetorical cliches and social tracts against the economic and political status quo, contemporary playwriting can be deeply disturbing. For these writers, "art becomes a statement of self-awareness — an awareness that presupposes a disharmony between the self of the artist and the community."[34] This alienation of the artist from the self and from the community makes artists into victims and at the same time calls them to violate the distance between the reader and the artwork.

STEPHEN HAPPEL

All the arts are dramatic action; to be authentic, they must prove brutal. Actors must train viscerally and physically as though they were dancers or athletes. Writers want pure theater, determined by the "physics of the absolute gesture, which is itself idea."[35] Dispensing with a previously written script, the actor must become the author, like a surgeon operating on a patient. Such explicit cruelty, without an anesthetic, is meant to excise cultural nightmares from the body politic.

This new mode of theater blends the differences between audience and actors, between life and art. Deeply interdisciplinary in practice, improvisation and methods, theater-work and life-work are meant to have an intimate relationship. The objective is to re-create not only a dialogue between culturally similar artifacts but to reinsert dramatic events within the rituals of life from which they emerge.

These dramatic tendencies have begun to examine Western theater's inner connections with daily rituals, religious sacraments and mythic retellings in dance and choreographic folk movements. For contemporary theater, the quest for the underlying foundations of human expression originates within the human body. "Our work is based on the fact that some of the deepest aspects of human experience can reveal themselves through sounds and movement of the human body in a way that strikes an identical chord in any observer, whatever his cultural conditioning."[36] The theater emphasizes the growth of the individual within community, an existential holism in union with the forces of the cosmos, and the political and personal transformation of the actors and audiences.[37] Disciplined artistic practice, akin to ritual preparation, leads beyond the self into an uncontrollable other, often encountered in an ecstatic, even trancelike state. The values espoused center on the genial individual whose originality has rejected the conventions of an artwork separated from life. In the case of contemporary theater, the self-expression of performance artists deliberately subverts any distinction between the personal life of the actors, the text being performed and the audience's individual or group identity.

THE INTERACTION OF TWO GENRES

Contemporary drama, therefore, is directed not to an audience but to a group of participants who share at some level in the activity of the actors. In addition, the entire ensemble is engaged in producing "something larger than themselves," so much so that there is a genuinely ecstatic invitation operative in good theater; hence, the usual presumption—that drama is addressed by a group of actors to a passive audience—is no longer in place. Actors and audience are participants in verbal and bodily actions that engage them at a quite visceral level. Both are addressing some other, even if unexpressed or inarticulately identified.

page 17

The shifts in the self-understanding of theater and drama have made the work of liturgists more difficult. In effect, the *forms* of nineteenth-century theater and liturgy shared a common bias about the relationship of performers to the audience: Art performed on one side of the proscenium was for the moral benefit of those on the other side, but interaction between the two was minimal. Just at the time theater moved in the direction of reintegrating itself within quotidian experience and into ecstatic pre-verbal rituals, contemporary Catholic liturgy after the Second Vatican Council chose more ordinary metaphors for its self-presentation. Latin gave way to vernacular speech; the shelf-like altar with its central, sacral tabernacle and visual altarpiece became a wooden or stone table across which the presider engaged the congregation; ritual gestures returned the presider to a dialogue with the congregation; liturgical clothing became simplified, often made of materials more like those of ordinary life; and liturgical utensils matched those of the family feast. Instead of the old self-effacing clerical activity in which "father" (with his back to the audience) prayed for the congregation to God, presiders in the United States now regularly introduce themselves in person and greet the assembly at various points in the service with ordinary, highly conversational exhortations. "Good morning, Father" is a typical response to an initial invitation. Drama discovered daily ritual, and liturgy found ordinary life.

So what can we say about the relationships between the *forms* of worship and drama at this point in our culture? First, we should recognize

STEPHEN HAPPEL

that the interaction between public religious rituals and theater performance is now as highly complex as it was when *Covenants* was originally performed in the fourteenth century! Dramatic actions have returned to the eucharistic ritual, but now in the ritual forms of ordinary life.

Second, eucharistic piety in many locations now encourages dramatic re-enactment during worship itself: enacted versions of the readings replace lectors; mimed versions of readings and prayers accompany readers and music; individuals (lay and clerical) give sermons or reflections on the readings while acting out the dialogues of the gospel; danced performances with music have returned as entrance processions, responsory psalms and as community participation at key moments during the eucharistic prayer. The catechetical demands of different interest groups, such as children or adolescents, even within one native language, have prompted numerous dramatic adaptations. Supertitles, such as those used over the proscenium in opera houses to translate foreign texts, have begun to replace hymnals in some churches.

In other words, the inherently dramatic nature of the eucharistic ritual has been reemphasized by the post–Vatican II church in some communities. The liturgy, however, like current drama, has taken two rather different dramatic paths: one *demotic* and the other *spectacular.* Using *demotic metaphors,* communities stress the familiar and familial, expressed through interpersonal gestures, actions and symbols (such as ordinary plates and bread, simple cups and wine, and less stylized vestments). Musical accompaniment tends to emerge from the talents of the congregation, however well- or ill-equipped. The familial, of course, often appears banal and flat by earlier standards of formal Catholic liturgy or when performed in larger churches.[38] Those communities for whom the *genre of the spectacle* dominates stress high technical artistic performance, trained actors for liturgical enactment and sometimes startling effects of lighting and sound. Since the *demotic* mode of eucharistic drama is more usually experienced, two examples of the *spectacular* drama in worship will illustrate what is meant.

On the weekend of Pope Paul VI's funeral in Rome, the Sunday eucharist at the Co-Cathedral in Las Vegas included an excellent African American vocalist dressed in a long white robe with gold sequins at the sleeves and throat. She was strikingly tall and walked across the sanctuary during the preparation of the gifts while singing into a hand-held micro-phone the popular song that begins "He . . . can turn the tides and calm the angry sea!" The music followed the pastor's counsel that poker chips were legal currency in the city and that worshipers should not think twice about putting them in the collection baskets. In effect, this latter *spectacular* mode used the high achievements of contemporary theater, partially to compete with the secular world of local entertainment.

page 19

A more effective example of spectacle, however, can be seen in a Sunday eucharist celebrated some years later at Oakland's old cathedral. The readings were Isaiah 55:10–11, which is about the effectiveness of God's word; Romans 8:18–23, in which the "sufferings of the present are nothing compared with the glory to be revealed"; and Matthew 13:1–23, the parable of the sower and the seed. The choir chose hymns about the word of God and hymns that used farming images. The entrance procession included dancers who threw imaginary seeds into the congregation while the presider followed with blessed water. The first reading was mimed by the dancer who, as it became clear, was deaf and mute; the second reading was completed by a blind African American who read by Braille; the gospel was begun by the deacon, who told the parable of the farmer going out to sow his seed, some on rocky ground, some on good soil. The two other readers, standing on either side of the deacon, asked, one in American Sign Language and one orally, "Why do you speak to them in parables?" The presider stepped for-ward and replied, "To you has been given a knowledge of the mysteries of the reign of God, but it has not been given to the others." The presider then completed the gospel reading with its allegorical explanations about words and seed, concluding (slightly out of textual sequence) with the following passage, first gesturing to the blind man on the right, then to the deaf man on the left: "Blest are your eyes because they see, and blest are your ears because they hear. I assure you, many a prophet and many a saint longed to see what you see but did not see it, to hear what you hear but did not hear it." The presider sat down. Complete silence occupied the crowded cathedral. The homily had been given.

Both the *demotic* and *spectacular* metaphoric initiatives, however, understand the liturgical structures as theatrical narratives, just as *Covenants* did. Both liturgical genres are simply dimensions of a popular culture that oscillates between the private, personal world of family or neighborhood rituals and the world outside the family, that of merchandized, manipulated public celebrations like the Super Bowl or a Las Vegas dinner show. Needless to say, family rituals and public celebrations cannot easily be separated in Western culture, precisely because both have been affected by advertising.

Interestingly enough, however, neither basic network of metaphors seems to reflect very much on the fact that they are engaged in a form of twentieth-century, post–Enlightenment inculturation of Christian liturgy not unlike that of *Covenants* in the fourteenth century. They are looking for the contemporary symbolic and rhetorical equivalents that will engage an audience, insert the congregation within the religious dimensions of their own culture and transform them as they go into the culture to act out their lives as Christians.

The two forms of dramatic rhetoric, *demotic* and *spectacular,* that largely inform Catholic eucharistic action and piety may not be the inventory from which we will choose the forms that will face the next millennium. However, they *are* the appeal being made within Catholic assemblies to the wider world. Evaluating the effectiveness of the forms as a rhetoric, discussing their appropriateness for the *content* of cooperation and self-sacrifice, determining what the criteria might be for making a judgment about their meaning and truth, are absolutely crucial theological (and hence cultural) tasks. Just as the late medieval discussions about the role of drama in worship created a distinct Western theater, so now it is critical to think carefully about how eucharistic inculturation is to occur in late-twentieth-century, post-industrial cultures. Excoriating these developing rhetorics because they are not the rhetoric of a Catholic Gothic or Baroque past will not be the most useful critique.

The *demotic* and *spectacular* metaphors chosen are meant, like *Covenants* in the Christian past, to convey moments of ultimacy and transcendence. They hope to challenge in some prophetic fashion the community's ability to "settle into" the culture without a gospel remainder. They want to announce to the culture that its worst evils may be changed or transformed, that God will effect change in the ordinary world.

page 21

This may be the most important question to ask of the current *demotic* and *spectacular* inculturations for eucharistic worship. It is easy to say that the new demotic and spectacular forms of Christian eucharist do not convey transcendence in the way the earlier styles of expression did. The Middle Ages emphasized the story of Christ's sacrifice mimed in rubrics, preached in sermons and emphasized in eucharistic theology; that history was celebrated in drama, whether liturgical or theatrical. The absolute commitment of God to creation in the death of Jesus was the covenant that Christians shared by their participation in the narrative structures of the eucharist and in the dramatic language of the stage. It is not quite so easy to say how the new forms, whether demotic or spectacular, might evoke the same experiences of ultimacy.

Inculturation and the issues of translation have been reflected on most often in the context of non–European cultures, since large-scale evangelization came from the colonializing West during the Renaissance and early modern period of its history. It is just as important, however, to think seriously about how the gospel and its liturgical context can be embodied in the world created by the secularity of the Enlightenment. None of the previous cultural expressions of Christianity "gave up" on their cultures. How does our church meet the cultural challenges of the present and virtual worlds? How do we explore the depths of our own cultures without either glorifying or trivializing these depths so that the dramatic entry of transcendence into our world may be conveyed?

page 22

       This is what Roland Reed's *Covenants* has challenged us to do. By reinterpreting the past rhetorical incursions of drama and music into worship, it makes us realize the risks that our medieval ancestors took when trying to experience, understand and embody the meanings of the eucharist. The same kind of risks must be taken by Christian communities in the present if they are to find a credible sacramental rhetoric for the next millennium.

Endnotes

1. All quotations from the plays are taken from *Covenants: A Cycle of Plays Covering Significant Events from the "Creation of Everything" to "The Nativity,"* adapted from the medieval mystery plays of the northern English towns of York, Wakefield, N-Town, and Chester and the Digby. © Ms. Roland Reed, 1988, 1995. The production was made possible by a generous grant from the Magi Foundation at Catholic University of America.

page 23

2. A videotape of the performance is available upon request. Contact Roland Reed, Department of Drama, Catholic University of America, Washington, D.C. 20064.

3. See a popular treatment of eucharistic development through artistic styles in music, the visual arts and architecture in Edward Foley, *From Age to Age: How Christians Have Celebrated the Eucharist* (Chicago: Liturgy Training Publications, 1991). See especially pp. 3–113.

4. Actors and apostates were both refused reconciliation at the Synod of Laodicea in the late fourth century. See Salvatore Paterno, *The Liturgical Context of Early European Drama* (Potomac, MD: Scripta Humanistica, 1989): 25–40.

5. See Johannes Quasten, *Music and Worship in Pagan and Christian Antiquity,* trans. Boniface Ramsey (Washington, D.C.: National Association of Pastoral Musicians, 1983). See especially pp. 121–128.

6. Lactantius, *Divine Institutes,* bk VI, ch. 20, cited in Paterno, *Liturgical Context,* pp. 10–11.

7. See Paul Corby Finney, *The Invisible God: The Earliest Christians on Art* (New York: Oxford University Press, 1994). See especially pp. 15–68. See also Frédérick Tristan, *Les Premières Images Chrétiennes: Du Symbole à L'icône, IIe-VIe s* (Paris: Fayard, 1996): 162–77.

8. For descriptions and some excerpts, see Paterno, *Liturgical Context,* 60–66. The interpretations in this volume, however, leave much to be desired.

9. For Amalarius of Metz discussed in the context of literature, see O.B. Hardison, Jr., *Christian Rite and Christian Drama in the Middle Ages: Essays in the Origin and Early History of Modern Drama* (Baltimore: Johns Hopkins Press, 1965): 47–77.

10. Sophronius, "Commentarius Liturgica," P.G., XLIVbis, ed. lat., col. 1136.

11. Ibid., cols. 1128–30.

12. See Hrabanus Maurus, "De Clericorum Institutione, P.L. 107, col. 324D.

13. Amalarius of Metz, *De Ecclesiasticis Officiis,* P.L. 105, col. 1112.

14. Bernold of Constance, *Micrologus de ecclesiasticis observationibus,* P.L. 151, col. 987.

15. Sandro Sticca, *The Latin Passion Play: Its Origin and Development* (Albany: State University of New York Press, 1970): 6. It is not clear that Hrotswitha's plays were ever acted in our modern sense of the term, although the farcical element in *Dulcitius* could function well as a staged mimic activity. It was not atypical in late antiquity to have stationary readers whose words were simultaneously mimed by actors.

16. *Concordia Regularis,* ed. Thomas Symonds (New York, 1953): 49–50, cited in Sticca, *Latin Passion Play,* p. 8.

17. See Richard B. Donovan, *The Liturgical Drama in Medieval Spain* (Toronto: Pontifical Institute of Mediaeval Studies, 1958): 13–14.

18. Ibid.: 55–56.

19. Ibid.: 35.

20. *Poetria Nova of Geoffrey of Vinsauf,* trans. Margaret F. Nims (Toronto: Pontifical Institute of Mediaeval Studies, 1967): 87–88.

21. Thomas Aquinas, *Summa Theologiae,* II–II, Q. 168, aa. 3–4. My translations.

22. See Johan Huizinga, *The Waning of the Middle Ages: A Study of the Forms of Life, Thought, and Art in France and the Netherlands in the XIVth and XVth Centuries* (New York: St. Martin's Press, 1967). See the setting of this emphasis upon sight and the elevation of the eucharist in its social context in John Bossy, *Christianity in the West: 1400–1700* (New York: Oxford University Press, 1985): 66–72, and Nathan Mitchell, *Cult and Controversy: The Worship of the Eucharist Outside Mass* (New York: Pueblo Publishing Co., 1982): 49–62, 97–104, 129–86.

23. See the description of their development in Miri Rubin, *Corpus Christi: The Eucharist in Late Medieval Culture* (Cambridge: Cambridge University Press, 1992). See especially pp. 271–87, 324–34.

24. Lauren Lepow, *Enacting the Sacrament: Counter-Lollardy in the Towneley Cycle* (London and Toronto: Associate University Presses, 1990): 24. My translation from the Middle English text.

25. Ibid.: 50.

26. These same themes are repeated in the altarpieces of late medieval churches. Their dramatic quality confirms the elaboration in both ritual and drama. See, for example, Barbara G. Lane, *The Altar and the Altarpiece: Sacramental Themes in Early Netherlandish Painting* (New York: Harper & Row, 1984): 79–136.

27. Ibid.: 55–62.

28. See Hans-Jürgen Diller, "Theological Doctrine and Popular Religion in the Mystery Plays," in *Religion in the Poetry and Drama of the Late Middle Ages in England,* ed. Piero Boitani and Anna Torti (Rochester, N.Y.: D.S. Brewer, 1990): 203. For philosophical reflections upon the role of testimony in truth-telling, see Paul Ricoeur, "The Hermeneutics of Testimony," in *Essays on Biblical Interpretation,* ed. Lewis S. Mudge (Philadelphia: Fortress Press, 1980): 119–54.

29. See the discussion of the York Creation and Fall of Lucifer, much like that in *Covenants,* by Richard Beadle, "Poetry, Theology and Drama in the York *Creation* and *Fall of Lucifer,*" in Boitani and Torti, *Religion in the Poetry and Drama,* pp. 213–27.

30. Hardison, *Christian Rite,* p. 79.

31. Ibid.: 284–92.

THE INTERACTION OF TWO GENRES

32. By *spectacular,* I mean highly organized, specialized performances that require a large outlay of resources, multiple actors, and sometimes showy results. The term *demotic* comes from the Greek *demos,* the people — a popular from of rhetoric, rooted in ordinary speech, the expressions of family life, friendship and the neighborhood. The terms are used descriptively, not pejoratively.

33. For a more complete overview of the development of western theater, see Stephen Happel, "The Arts as a Matrix of Spiritual Experience: Frederick Hart's *Three Soldiers* and the Vietnam Veterans Memorial," in *Spirituality and the Secular Quest,* ed. Peter H. Van Ness (New York: Crossroad, 1996).

page 25

34. Susan Sontag, "Antonin Artaud," in *Antonin Artaud: Selected Writings,* ed. Susan Sontag, trans. Helen Weaver (New York: Farrar, Straus and Giroux, 1976): xix.

35. Ibid.: xxxii.

36. Peter Brook, "On Africa: Interview with Peter Brook," *Drama Review* 17 (1973), 3:50 cited in Richard Schechner, *Between Theater & Anthropology* (Philadelphia, PA.: University of Pennsylvania Press, 1985): 27.

37. See T.J. Scheff, *Catharsis in Healing, Ritual, and Drama* (Berkeley, CA: University of California Press, 1979).

38. Much of the critique of current Catholic music and architecture, for example, in Thomas Day, *Why Catholics Can't Sing: The Culture of Catholicism and the Triumph of Bad Taste* (New York: Crossroad, 1990), originates as a problem not so much about faith as about cultural adaptation. M. Francis Mannion argues for attention to musical classics in the Western tradition of the Catholic church, lest the community lose its history and identity. The paradigms he offers embody metaphoric and cultural differences. How the relative merits of cultural embodiments are to be evaluated will require a complex socio-cultural analysis. Whether there are genuinely *theological* differences within the paradigms remains to be studied. See M. Francis Mannion, "Paradigms in American Catholic Church Music," *Worship* 70:2 (March 1996): 101–128.

A Prophetic Eucharist
in a Prophetic Church

DAVID N. POWER, OMI

As we move toward the third millennium of Christianity, the catchphrase in ecclesial circles is "the new evangelization," a term that points both to a renewed energy in spreading the gospel and to a spiritual revival of lived fidelity in traditionally Christian countries. Much in use since around 1980, it is clear, however, that the term has been given quite varied interpretations, ranging from promoting a neo-conservatism of rigorous church structure to strong apocalyptic expectations.

The particular accent this presentation gives to the work of evangelization as we head into the next millennium is found in the word prophetic.[1] It is picked out not only as a mark of church witness but also as a characteristic that can allow the celebration of the eucharist to evolve at its heart.

The Prophetic

The nature and power of the prophetic is suggested in the narrative of the Pentecostal event in the Book of Acts. The testimony to the death and resurrection of Jesus Christ that the faithful gave on that day and thereafter is portrayed as the breaking forth of energies inherent among the people, with no exception of age or person. In its varied forms, this testimony emerged from a new effusion of God's Spirit. It pointed to the kerygma of the death and resurrection of Jesus Christ as God's Word and to the testimony of the believers as the action of the Spirit. In its richness, it anticipated a new age, the coming of God's rule in fidelity to the covenant built on the twin commandments of love of God and love of neighbor. Those who acted prophetically gave witness by their lives, words and actions to the power which this paschal event had in their midst and to the promises that it held forth. Proclaimed as God's decisive historical intervention in human and cosmic history, the Pasch as proclaimed on that day of the first Pentecost holds immense potentialities to transform life, but these have to be spelled out for any given time through new prophetic proclamation, challenge and interpretation.

To be prophetic in any age is to look back to Pentecost and forward to a time when, in life, institution and ritual, the churches will be able, in the name of witnessing to Christ, to witness to the hope of a new humanity by being a catalyst for changing society among peoples. To be a prophetic community is to preach afresh the gospel as God's living Word. It is to discern and to highlight the newly creative actions of the Spirit in the church and in the world. It is to live from the presence and power of the Spirit at work in all the people, without discrimination, opposition or fracturing. In times of social and cultural crisis and oppression, the Body of Christ is called to portray the life of an alternative humanity in which God's Spirit works, overcoming the death-dealing forces abroad in the world. Far from claiming a monopoly of spiritual energy within itself, it assumes a prophetic role as it reads the signs of the times, showing what needs are to be faced, what energies are abroad and to what humanity the gospel is to be proclaimed.

Royal Consciousness and the Prophetic

page 29

The prophetic challenge of the Christian community is in the first place to society and the community of nations. Inspired by the gospel and the living memory of Jesus Christ, Christians — even in pluralistic societies — must speak for values not widely respected and for persons too often neglected. This they do as they look on life with the eyes of faith and with trust in the God of Jesus Christ, who is pure love and pure gift.

The life-giving force that allows this projection of a new humanity, however, is impossible unless churches break with inert forms of behavior, rule and ritual, and give rein to often fettered life-forces. The works of Walter Brueggemann, beginning with his book *The Prophetic Imagination*,[2] have served well on this continent in framing an understanding of the prophetic. His use of the expressions "prophetic," "prophetic consciousness" and "prophetic imagination" has been quite widely adopted. It must be admitted that this is done in different contexts and to different purposes, some more favorable to change and some more compelled by a need to return to abandoned expressions of the holy.

In using the terminology here, one factor that is underlined is the contrast that Brueggemann makes between royal consciousness and prophetic consciousness, applying it to both ecclesiastical and civic realities. In pithy terms, royal consciousness is a confidence in established institutions and traditions which are canonized, or turned into a canon, as the embodiment of the ideal. They are thus defended against intrusion or innovation. This canonical mentality is found at present within the field of literature, as for example in the opposition to the inclusion of African American literature or Hispanic literature in the curriculum of a school or college, lest they challenge the prevailing sense of the moral and the appropriate. It is found in the field of politics in many of the appeals against affirmative action in the name of the Constitution. It is found in the church whenever criticism of the pope or a bishop is considered an affront to Jesus Christ, or in some of the talk about resacralizing the liturgy by a return to old forms of language and rite.

It is one of the signs of the times that this royal consciousness is breaking down by virtue of its own internal inadequacies. Politically, despite the efforts of great powers to spread their civic and economic ideals, we see the breakdown of world community, the staying power or the emergence of forces of violence and injustice, and the spread of what has been called by way of oxymoron a culture of death and disbelief. On a positive side, but in the pangs of struggle, we witness the challenge to foster a more just global economy and a cultural pluralism of broad exchange.

The breakdown of royal consciousness, due to loss of confidence in institutions and traditions, is widespread in society. More dramatically for those of us who are Catholics, it is found in the church in teachings, institutions and liturgies that find little response among the faithful. That there is some legitimacy and need for the critique of institutions is acknowledged within the institutions themselves, as witness several recent papal apologies. Addressing remarks to the assembly of Latin American bishops meeting at Santo Domingo in 1992, Pope John Paul asked the forgiveness of Indian and African American peoples for the belittlement and domination of their respective cultures at the time of the conquest and since.[3] In 1995, the same pope, while certainly not fully satisfying every woman's desire for inclusion, nonetheless felt compelled in the name of the very gospel that is core to his call for a new evangelization to apologize to women for their long-term oppression and exclusion within the life of the church.[4] This happens not only in male attitudes but even in hierarchical and ritual prescription. In that same year, addressing other ecclesial bodies, he acknowledged inadequacies in the papacy that block full communion between churches.[5] If these statements are not a challenge to royal consciousness at the very heart of the church institution, what are they?

Prophetic Shape of the Eucharist

If there is one place in the church where the prophetic consciousness needs *page 31* to be given voice and expression, it is within the commemoration of Christ's death and resurrection, in the rite that claims its birth at the table of the prophetic Last Supper. In keeping the memorial of the Pasch of Christ and of the outpouring of the Spirit, the church is assured of Christ's active presence, of his love for the poor of the earth and of the continued sacramental gift of himself and of the Spirit. It continues to hear and be challenged by the gospel of discipleship. Drawing life from within its liturgical gathering, the church in its membership can speak with a prophetic voice in the shaping of society, in the assurance of a divine love and a divine generosity that is beyond measure, and of a divine justice beyond all human justice.

When the liturgy validates hope for the church community, it can speak in public for this hope both corporately and in its individual members. When the liturgy symbolizes and confirms a vision of humanity, of human relations and of transcendental values, the public stance of Christians is motivated and inspired. What it expresses of attitudes to individuals, to the poor, to those unjustly treated or to minorities can be integrated into the public language and action of believers. If the eucharistic liturgy itself beclouds Christ's vision or suppresses charismatic and prophetic voices, individual Christians may continue to act out of their persuasions and convictions; but they must do so without the affirmation and support of the church community.

The forms for a prophetic eucharist that engender prophetic presence are first learned from the way we remember the supper of Jesus and the disciples. When *Societas Liturgica* met in Dublin in August 1995 to commemorate the fiftieth anniversary of Gregory Dix's *Shape of the Eucharist,* it discussed this shape in anticipation of the future. In doing this, there is some danger of being tied too narrowly to a ritual shape or cursus ascribed to New Testament texts. Ritual needs to be examined in light of the message proclaimed and the gift given.

In reforming the celebration of the eucharist in the light of the New Testament shape, the prophetic actions and words of Jesus at supper must be allowed to stand forth in bold relief; they suggest a prophetic shape for the coming of the millennium.[6] Several elements of this table action are pertinent to the ongoing prophetic character of the church's eucharist:

> a. As narrated in the scriptures, in word, action, prayer, promise and gift, Jesus himself pointed to his death as the decisive moment of God's intervention. As he proclaimed it, this brought to fulfilment a historic sequence of events in which humankind, and especially Israel, had been befriended by the gracious action of the divine creative and liberating Spirit. From its place in this history, it would open up a future to be lived out through time, until the eschaton.

> b. Most important of all, the sacrament of presence and promise is a table at which the blessings, the commemorative eating of the lamb and the prescribed ritual flow all give way to the awesome act of gift, the gift given in the anxiety of the morrow's anticipation. While Jesus blessed God in remembrance of divine works and in interpreting ancient symbols in anticipation of his own death, he did it so that he might give himself, through the blessing in God's power, as food and drink to his disciples.

> c. The table thus to be dressed was one to which access was given through the washing of feet, where the master took the role of the slave, and in performing that action uttered a new commandment for his disciples.

d. The self-giving, the fearsome anticipation of broken body and blood poured out, voiced first in words of blessing, was conclusively expressed in the breaking of the bread and the distribution of the cup among table fellows.

e. The worship thus rendered to God was without inner sanctum to which the priest withdrew. It was worship in spirit and in truth. It was in worship wherein God's giving and Christ's giving were in the forefront, rather than the formalities of a cult addressed to God. Henceforth, obedience to the law could only be the obedience to the gospel of the suffering servant. Whoever prays at this table must be as one who serves, and whoever drinks of the cup must drink of it to the dregs of self-giving, that others may have life.

page 33

f. This action may well be related back to the concerns of the traders in the temple rebuked by Christ for their concern with the approved money, and the allotted pots and pans, that were to be allowed into the holy of Yahweh (John 2:13–17). Such concerns were set aside in the choice of the raw materials of this common table, which were the raw materials of a life of work in tilling the earth.

g. When the gospels relate this supper table to the table actions of Jesus throughout his life, or to his feeding of the crowds, it appears as a table open to the forgotten and the misbegotten, a table well fitted to the prophetic community that heeds the voice of those who seek food in their hunger, consolation in their pain, reconciliation in their alienation.

These few points enable us to formulate more readily a prophetic reading of the supper narrative and its pertinence to the eucharist. Some commentators point to the actions of Jesus in breaking the bread and pouring the cup as prophetic, and various ideas can center around this. First, the designation is given to these actions because they imitate the Old Testament prophets who on occasion acted out the message of God before the eyes of the people. Second, by dint of this comparison, the prophetic quality of Jesus's actions stands out as a proclamation of God's presence, action and promise, connected with the event of his death. Third, it shows how Jesus, not only in action but in word, was able to relate this presence to a covenantal tradition, pointing at the same time to continuity in God's fidelity and to a definitive moment of its realization. Fourth, it reveals how Jesus himself accepted and then transmitted God's grace, in word and sign, through an act of thanksgiving. Out of the hope and reverence born of this thanksgiving, he committed himself to letting his own life and being, and his very death, be the place where God's action takes hold in the world. Fifth, in associating prophecy and proclamation with table bread and wine, Jesus transformed the worship of God by letting all the power and imagery of cult pour into these simple things and actions, thus generating a worship in spirit and in truth. Sixth, by inviting the disciples into communion with himself in the new commandment of service, and in the communion of life through the gift of his body and blood, he made of the supper, or eucharist, a prophetic act to be continued in the life of his disciples.

Eucharist, Prophetic and Royal Consciousness

When this prophetic consciousness is brought to the celebration of the Lord's table, this age can find therein the urge to renew the forms of word and rite. Renewal of forms is not possible without the critique of established forms, however, especially when these are affected by inordinate attachment to institutional niceties.

One of the obstacles to a good celebration of the eucharist is its overidentification with sacred ritual, the loss of the words and the acts born in the freedom of the Spirit to express communion among participants. Of its nature the eucharist has key ritual moments and incorporates many ritual actions, but it is beyond ritual. Ritual, when set down by authority and invested with the esteem of the congregation, fixes horizons and attitudes and gives specific words and actions the quality of the sacred. The central acts of the sacrament are indeed such a rite, but they are set within a larger celebration.

page 35

Eucharist is ritual with a story and logic of action that moves "out of" the story. The logic of the action is inspired by the story but must move into another story, the story of the people gathered. Fixing attention on a moment or symbol of sacred presence obscures the kind of representation given by the recall of the story of the Passion or of the deeds of Christ. This invites hearers to a way of being that takes issue with the forces of darkness and death. It is a story that is remembered and represented in the liturgy not only in one mode but in a variety of narratives that intertwine and challenge. What is called for in memorial is not a formal or ritualistic configuration of the Christ who is remembered; it is rather a participation in his story and its truth that calls on Christians to situate themselves in relation to life and its challenge in virtue of how they see themselves living and acting from their internalization of what the story expresses. The prophetic word is in dialectic with the symbolic rite of representation and with the sacred text of a once-for-ever narrative proclamation. It is the dialectic of remembered history, actuating symbol and the moment to be here and now lived in faith.

The prophetic word as a word that deciphers the challenges and the possibilities of the present comes then from the members of the community, who listen and speak in the power of the Spirit. There has always been room in eucharistic celebration for a word that is not pre-fixed, for a challenge to stabilized vision and ethic in the listening to the gospel and in the evocation of Christ's memory. Traditionally this has occurred within the homily, in the free proclamation of traditional texts or in prayers that have no set form. In the New Testament church, the meal gathering at which the eucharist was celebrated allowed for the deployment of charisms and the proclamation of prophetic voices. The extent to which some speech and some action in eucharistic gatherings were of free composition changed over time. There is, however, by the nature of this assembly, a place built in for prophetic challenge to established ways of hearing the gospel, to conceiving the church or to enunciating an evangelical ethic in regard to current affairs and human policies.

This challenge can be given and heard in some measure even within the pattern of the present Roman Missal. The presider can exercise evangelical freedom at various points in the celebration. First and foremost, with help from members of the community in its preparation, he can in the homily let the biblical and gospel word address the assembly in a prophetic way. There are several points of intervention open to him at which this word can be given ritual context, as in the penitential prayer, the introduction to the eucharistic prayer or the invitation to the common recital of the Lord's Prayer. At different points in the Mass, voices can also be heard from other members of the assembly, as in the introduction to the readings, the prayer of the faithful and shared moments of reflection at the beginning of the celebration or before the final blessing. All of this requires thought and reflection, both on the scriptures and on life's witness, for like some homilies, any intervention by any person can be sheer meandering. The belief and experience of the gifts of the Spirit, however, together with the conviction of the value of the witness given to Christ's Pasch in many a life, can lead assemblies to more than this.

The purpose of such interventions is to move the community from the written text to oral exchange within which persons address persons in virtue of a common memory and a shared life. They bring the assembly from the once-for-all event of the Pasch remembered in ritual to the historical moment, in which the hope engendered is to be lived out. They move beyond the paradigmatic story to the living out of that story in concrete circumstances where choices are made.

When inertia sets in, the critique of royal consciousness and the emergence of a prophetic word within liturgy are not primarily done at desks. They go on in the midst of those who are seeking new ways of being church, who are asking a word from God in the face of human dilemmas or who feel disaffected with the church. Critique and prophecy emerge through creativity in the rites to which communities give birth, drawing on Christian imagination and on their own ways of expressing the power of the Spirit that they know from experience. Countering the ritual forms that have burdened and asphyxiated means giving place to the ritualization born from life and from the capacity to be inventive in drawing on what is most powerful in the gift of Christ — even where, from a formal point of view, the rite is truncated. Countering the silence to which the Word has been reduced through the inhibition of its forms of proclamation, assemblies of faithful gather in the witness of the Spirit heard in the hearts of disciples of all walks of life. Looking back to the prophetic shape of the supper challenges the church today to both a prophetic ritual-breaking in its form and action, and a prophetic proclamation. It attends to whatever word speaks to what it is to live out current affairs in the memory of the Christ of table and cross, in whose presence among them by his sacramental gift of self the community of disciples firmly believes.

When some communities, with or without ordained members, go against the rules, their celebration is not necessarily flamboyance or gross irregularity. They are in fact trying to connect, fitting their own reality, distress and hope into the catholic reality. They work with traditional and familiar rituals but are experimenting with them somewhat to see how it is possible to find new ways of being evangelical, Christian and catholic. Of course, at times these efforts do not succeed, are short-lived or in fact create anarchy. What is needed in such cases is not condemnation but a ready ear for what is being said and sought as well as empathy, dialogue and constructive guidance.

Community Eucharist Led by the Baptized

Ritually, there are many anomalies in the life of the church at present. The participation of all the baptized without discrimination, and especially the

DAVID N. POWER, OMI

participation of women and the more humbly educated, has not yet been achieved. An increasing number of communities cannot have a Sunday eucharist presided by an ordained minister. In other respects, as in the celebration of baptism, marriage or a funeral, they have ritually vibrant gatherings but are faced with the dilemma of how to fashion their Sunday worship.

The reality and the worship of such "dis-ordered" communities, to use a play on words, is in fact a possible starting point for revitalization. We must look not just at what they are not, but at what they are. In other words, there is merit in looking to the eschatological sign of assemblies "without order" but in which sacrament is celebrated, offered, taken and shared in the generous, mutual, Spirit-filled, sharing of selves. Compared with episcopal liturgies, these may seem sparse or dis-ordered, but they allow for the washing of feet, for pentecostal voices, for words and stories exchanged, for witness given, for a bread sharing of divine giving. Sacramentality is at work in their remembrance of Jesus Christ and in the breath of God's Spirit. Cultural and local patterns that will help shape the future of the church and its worship may, in time, emerge from such efforts.

The reality of Sunday assemblies presided over by persons other than an ordained presider has become a reality today in North America and in Europe, and it tends to be looked upon as a "problem." Because it has appeared now on the dominant continents of the world, it is getting new attention. Let us not forget that this has been a reality for a long time on other continents and that the people of other climes and cultures nonetheless give strong evidence of being living and worshiping communities.

The issue at stake is not that of holding communion services as such, for these are a common factor in many ecclesial traditions. What is questioned is their dominance as the form of Sunday service in some gatherings. Faced with this possibility, many liturgists and theologians voice the opinion that the policy of ordination needs to change. That seems self-evident, even if, oddly, it is not admitted, because perhaps the determining focus is on ideas and structures of power, not on communities of faith.

To dwell on the discussion of ordination, however, is to pass over the here and now. The practice of ordination will, we hope, change, but it probably will not in an immediately foreseeable future and may change in directions possibly unknown to us yet. Long-term change is given slow birth amid both hope and travail. In the meantime, whatever is augured for the future, such communities continue to gather. It does not seem proper that local churches be forbidden the gift of Christ's sacrament in the name of policy or liturgical ideal; imaginative thought has to be given from within these communities to the rite whereby their eucharist is celebrated as a communion in Christ and his Spirit, within the communion of apostolic churches.[7]

page 39

The relation between blessing or eucharistic prayer and the sharing in the gift in the *koinonia* of the table needs reconsideration. Because there is a renewed accent in liturgical history and practice on the importance of the table prayer and on the participation of all the baptized in it, there is also renewed emphasis on the *action*. This action is fundamentally one of thanksgiving, and in traditional terms the sacrifice of the church is primarily the church's share in Christ's own thanksgiving. It is also, however, described as a sacrifice in the bread and wine, in which the things of life are blessed and transformed by the power of the Spirit. Much can be made of the importance of the sequence of offering and blessing that precedes the act of communion within the one liturgical gathering.

Nonetheless, the primacy of Christ's gift, the desire to make this gift available to all his disciples and companions, and the gratuity of this gift are not to be obscured. Even if it has to be done through alternative rites, the primary pastoral choice ought to be to make the sacrament as available as possible to the faithful, here and now, even while awaiting the ultimate resolution in a change of ordination polity. There is no point in telling communities that their members ought to displace themselves by going to other churches to get Mass. With some ritual imagination, community-based communion services can be celebrated appropriately without violating either the nature of the sacrament or the apostolic communion between churches.

DAVID N. POWER, OMI

In gatherings of the baptized "without order," there is ample room for word, thanksgiving, intercession and table-sharing all done in memorial of Christ's Pasch and in joyful reception of his gift. Because each such community is united in apostolic communion with another community where an ordained minister presides, it can be ritually given a relation to that community based on the analogy of a station or titular church to a primary church.[8] At the end of a Sunday liturgy, the community could ritually send its own gifts, inclusive of bread and wine and gifts for the poor, to the primary church and its community. At the vigil (Saturday evening) Mass in the primary church, these gifts could be presented to the assembly by a representative of the station community, with request for a blessing. They could then be ritually sent by the primary community and ritually received by the station community the following Sunday morning.

In some such liturgical action, three purposes are served. The primary one is that the sacrament is made available to all, even if with altered rites. The second is that the integrity and eucharistic reality of a community of baptized is recognized, with its Spirit-endowed power to gather and celebrate in memory of Christ; it has its own inner power to read and proclaim the word, offer sacrifice of thanksgiving to God, gather gifts for the poor, mutually comfort and enlighten, and share together at the table prepared by Christ. Third, by the ritual performance of sharing between communities, the sense of being united by order in one greater communion is kept, and the risk of treating the sacramental species as a thing to be kept in reserve for occasional use is avoided.

While it is regrettable that it is necessary to leave communities without ordained ministers, the new experience and celebration of communities who "swap communion services" is offering the church new insight into sacramentality. It incorporates the ministerial roles of the baptized, assembly and individuals, and leads all to be more aware of the great gift that Christ gives the church in the sacrament of his body and blood, shared together at table. It also brings out a meaning of the sacrament of order that is not reducible to the power to confect sacraments but illustrates that it is intended to serve unity in apostolic faith and a common eucharistic sharing.[9] This is an important implication given the long centuries through which ordination was viewed primarily as a conferral of sacramental power, many times placed out of ecclesial context.

page 41

Critique of Language and Ritual

In keeping with this practice, an obstacle to renewal and to evangelical testimony is in fact found in the language, practice and polity of sacramental power. The Western Roman Catholic church has never fully overcome the priestly dominance of which Martin Luther accused it when he pointed to the overshadowing of the word by ritual, of the people by the priest and of the gift of the sacrament by the action of sacrifice.[10] The first of his criticisms has been addressed by the role given to the proclamation of the word in the revised Roman liturgy, the second by promoting the active and conscious participation of all the baptized in the Mass, and the third by a more frequent practice of taking communion at the Lord's table. There are still factors, however, in language and in practice that impede a full sacramental representation of communion in Christ and the Spirit. In a climate of ecumenical mutual recognition there is an opportunity to internalize Luther's critique more fully, learning from both the liturgy and the theology of other churches.

Too many questions are addressed by some today, whether ecclesiastical authorities or liturgists, by looking at the action of the priest instead of at the proclamation of the word, the giving of the gift and the table action of the community, which includes blessing and sacramental communion. Mary Collins has discussed the language of ministry, with its emphasis on power, order, hierarchy and the sacred, that leads to distinctions in the body of the church that are stronger than the sense of communion and participation that by gospel right mark the body of Christ.[11]

There are vestiges of this kind of language in the 1975 *General Instruction of the Roman Missal* (GIRM). While the institution of the eucharist at the paschal supper is recalled, it is defined in essence as the sacrifice of Christ's body and blood (GIRM, introduction, 1). The sacramental performance of this sacrifice is attributed to the ordained bishop or presbyter (introduction, 4), while the participation of the faithful is called a spiritual sacrifice, offered through the priest (introduction, 5). To the priest is attributed action *in persona Christi* (introduction, 4; chapter 2, 7), granted that elsewhere the real presence of Christ in the assembly is affirmed *(Christus realiter praesens adest in ipso coetu)* (GIRM, 7) and a variety of ministries are given provision. Traditionally, the term *in persona Christi* meant simply that the sacramental action is efficacious by reason of the power of Christ, not by that of the person of the minister. It has become overloaded with such representational imagery over time that its continued usage suggests strong distinctions within the body. This is accentuated by the distinction between the sacramental sacrifice offered by the priest and the spiritual sacrifice of the people, a distinction that bypasses the sacramental nature and action of the liturgical assembly as such.[12] There is also some confusion about the role of the priest in the assembly of the local church, to which Christ's promises apply particularly (GIRM, chapter 2, 7), and the priest's role as minister of the universal church. The instruction states that the celebration of the Mass is the center of life for both the universal and the local church (GIRM, chapter 1, 1), which is, of course, a common tenet of Christian tradition; however, it seems to be, because of a direct relation of the priest to Christ and to the universal church, that celebration by a priest without an assembly is still seen as a possibility (GIRM, chapter 1, 4). This confuses the relation between local church and universal church, and places the ordained priest to some extent outside the local church for which he is ordained.

The nature of the eucharist as a table communion, a communal memorial of the body formed as one by Christ's Spirit and an ecclesial participation in Christ's sacrifice, is obscured by these linguistic and organizational distinctions. Needless to say, the distinction is accentuated by the all-too-frequent ritual practice of giving communion to the faithful in the sacramental species of the bread alone. It is further heightened by concele-brations that lack balance between clergy and baptized or by the continua-tion of the stipendiary system of private Masses for private intentions. For a truly prophetic celebration of the eucharistic memorial, the relation between eucharist and community and its place within the shaping of the local church needs to be given clearer formulation and priority over the individ-ual acts of ministers.

page 43

A further critique of eucharistic practice has to do with the accen-tuation of sacrifice that blurs sacrament and gift. Even in the renewed liturgy, when the importance of the great thanksgiving prayer is rightly underlined, Catholic theology tends to emphasize the ecclesial action of offering sacri-fice more than the receiving of the gift of Christ's body and blood with thanksgiving. In early tradition, it was precisely as an act of thanksgiving that the blessing prayer over the table was called a sacrifice. Whatever the merits of the ecumenical retrieval of the eucharistic prayer, to be fully prophetic the church stands in need of the retrieval of a table where the focus is again on gift. The *gift*—of God's love, of Christ, of Spirit, of one to the other, enfleshed and bestowed with promise — is the central image, not the sacrificial action of the church. It is in the giving of the gift, indeed with blessing, that the sac-rifice of Christ is in the first place sacramentally renewed. We must learn anew that what count is not what is *done* but what God gives and humans receive.

Shaping Eucharist and the Signs of the Times

This demythologization of the language of power, offering and sacrifice is integral to the critique of royal consciousness, which frees the way for pro-phetic vision. Beyond the critique, the signs of the times demand of the Catholic church that, in the renewal of its adherence to Jesus Christ and in its eucharistic gathering, it find ways to incorporate vital new energies and ritual forms. This is but to openly acknowledge and exercise the gifts of the Spirit, often working in unexpected ways. It is to affirm and integrate these movements of the Spirit into the proclamation of the death of Jesus Christ until his coming so that they can be carried over into the ethical domain of public life.

To be briefly programmatic about what can affect eucharistic celebration in light of the signs of the times as the churches look outside themselves, one must allude to the following needs:

a. An incorporation needs to be made of memories, voices, actions and symbols that—to appeal to Julia Kristeva's thought when she discusses the situation of women in church and society—have been relegated to the undertow of communal and cultural life rather than given expression in the symbolic order.[13] This is not only for the sake of allowing a legitimate place to the excluded but for the sake of finding a fuller symbolic expression that takes in the whole of human life and the communal but varied human reality. The place of women, their experience and their ways of imaging reality have to be given primary attention, as Pope John Paul II himself has recognized; however, much more care needs to be given to the symbolic expression used in justifying the restriction of ordination to males.

The letter *Ordinatio Sacerdotalis* repeats the injunction but has omitted the kind of gender imagery used hitherto to give it reason.[14] Indeed, the letter greatly insists on the full participation of women in the life of the church and wants to state clearly that exclusion from ordination does not derogate from women's dignity. This itself is an invitation to seek other ways of imaging participation in the act of worship and representation of Christ, and the invitation has to be risked without fear of what it may reveal. All the praises in the world may be heaped upon Mary and upon women, but they cannot counter a liturgical action that is justified by a symbol system that employs imagery that says that when the community gathers, men alone may image Christ.[15]

page 45

Acknowledging the marginal affects not only the place and ministries of women. Rite and prayer also have to take light and vivacity from the life and imagery of other groups to which eucharistic liturgy traditionally gives surprisingly little attention. Such are the sick, the dying, the work-deprived, persons with disabilities[16] and children. Not only do they have a right to be present, but the rite and symbolic imagery of the celebration needs to embrace them within its representation of the body of Christ.[17] If the biblical remembrance of Jesus' own table were robustly incorporated into the eucharist, the ritual ordering of the assembly would be affected.

b. It is often noted that the Catholic eucharist fails to incorporate wonder over nature or blessing for the things of the earth, and hence fails to generate ecological consciousness. Considering the roots in nature of traditional biblical and paschal imagery, this is odd but true. Partly, the failure is due to a camouflaging of the elements of bread and wine, as well as to the fact that the bread and wine put on the table are frequently not provided from the stock of the persons present or are given unaccompanied by gifts for the needy. It is also partly due to a loss of earthy imagery, which is allied on the one hand to a Catholic notion of sin and on the other to the artificiality of the urbanization of life. As learners from cultures that Christianity has dominated over centuries,[18] church

communities could embody in liturgy the power of traditional cultures that have not been well-integrated into
the church's ritual, especially as they reflect the relationship between the human and the earth and between
the living and the dead.

c. Too often, teaching and practice seem to exclude from
the Lord's table the voice of human pain. Participants
are either counselled to offer up their suffering in patient
acceptance or are exhorted to rejoice in the victory of
Christ's death and in his resurrection. This is to forget
that Christ's own eucharist and gift arose from his pained
but loving look at humanity and from the anxious anticipation of the morrow's doom. The gift of himself in
sacrament was and is certainly a comfort, a strength, a
bestowal of the Spirit and an eschatological first-fruits. It
is, however, also the sacramental mode whereby Christ is
with his people in their pain and his way of praying with
them through the Spirit in their pain. It is from within
and out of that pain that the faithful, too, can find the
readiness of self-gift and the hope of life's victory over
death, something that is quite different from patient
acceptance. If the pain is not named and given voice, it
is only suppressed or sublimated.

d. The Catholic church has to go further in giving a living
recognition to the integrity of the Lord's supper and holy
communion in other churches. It is time to move beyond
agreed doctrinal statements to an actual affirmation of
the gift of Christ's body and blood and the sacrament of
the gift of the Spirit proclaimed and shared in other
Christian churches. Even if we remain short of gathering

at the one table, for reasons shared with the Orthodox churches, when we stop doubting the eucharistic truth and reality of Protestant churches we can be strengthened and enlightened by their practice in our own.

Conclusion

These are schematic notes intended to raise the issues that lie ahead, to attend to the energies of renewal that are at work. The cue was taken from the narrative of the day of Pentecost in the Book of Acts and from Walter Brueggemann's *Prophetic Imagination.* Prophetic ministry, as he notes, is ministry to the world, beginning with ministry in and to the body of believers. It offers the vision of an alternative humanity built in the power of the Spirit and in the joy of God's rule. It confronts the deadly and energizes for the future in the discovery and release of forces at work in the world and within the community. I have been concerned to note how the eucharist of Christ's body may act as an energizing force whereby, as at Pentecost, all God's people may find voice through the outpouring of the Spirit to give witness to the Pasch of Christ, in which sin and death are overcome and life prevails.

Through the power of the Spirit, we are given the hope that we may celebrate the eucharist anew, as a life-giving force that opens us to the challenge of proclaiming the gospel for the turn of the millennium. In its celebration, the church grasps anew the memorial of Christ's passion, couching it in the forms of a messianic and prophetic christology. In this memory, the church is emboldened in the Spirit to face the loss, the injustice, the inequality and the violence of the times as it embodies the fresh urgency of life breaking out and spilled out. This means opening worship to the human, to the flawed human, to human pain. As a prophetic act, the eucharist embodies the cry of Jesus himself in his own *eucharistia.* For this, the celebration of the eucharist has to be opened to the signs of the times, to the cry of the poor, to the need for a global social justice, to the victimization of cultures, persons, women and minorities, throughout the ages and in the present.

DAVID N. POWER, OMI

Those who make eucharist over the bread and wine to be shared must dare to name the grief, the sorrow of victims and even the disenchantment with the royal consciousness that impedes the freedom of the Spirit. Within congregations, a place is to be allowed to the voices of prophets who know how to acclaim the gift of Christ's pained body and of the Spirit, of memories suppressed but now brought to life, of energies denied but now breaking forth. Within this circle, there will even be a place for the acknowledgment of the energies and life-giving forces that are at work in peoples of other religious traditions,[19] and of the cultural forces that are shaping the world toward a humanity of diversified but global communion formed in peace and justice.

Endnotes

1. This could seem at first like explaining the obscure through the more obscure, given discussions about the nature of prophetic gifts in the New Testament. The explanation of the word given here depends on relating the New Testament manifestations to the actions and words of prophets in the Old Testament.

2. Walter Brueggemann, *The Prophetic Imagination* (Philadelphia: Fortress Press, 1983).

3. John Paul II, General Audience, Rome, October 21, 1992. In *L'Osservatore Romano,* weekly edition in English (October 28, 1992): N. 43 (1263) 11.

page 49

4. John Paul II, "Letter to Women," *Origins* 25/9 (1995): 137–43, especially 139.

5. John Paul II, "Encyclical *Ut Unum Sint,*" *Origins* 25/4 (1995): 49–72, especially 69–70.

6. David Power, *The Eucharistic Mystery: Revitalizing the Tradition* (New York: Crossroad, 1992): 23–65.

7. The Directory provides some norms and the groundwork from which to start. Authentic and true ritual is possible, where the realities of the situation are given expression. See Congregation for Divine Worship, *Directory for Sunday Celebrations in the Absence of a Priest,* translated by ICEL (Washington, D.C.: USCC Publications Office, 1988).

8. The analogy is with the titles and station churches of early Christian Rome. According to this plan, the bishop sent presbyters to celebrate in the titles around the city, sent the *fermentum* from the episcopal eucharist through the service of acolytes, and made occasional visits to the stations for the celebration of liturgy. Today, the question is what other rites would appropriately express this new "ritual field" of communion between churches, as well as serve the availability of the sacrament to all.

9. When it is asked whether the baptized of themselves, and in virtue of their own memorial prayer in the Spirit, can celebrate a eucharist, arguments are forwarded to favor such a theory. However, what is pointed out here is that the sacrament of order cannot be reduced to the power to confect the sacrament. The role of order is to broaden and gather into unity and communion the many communities of faith and worship, where the name of Jesus and the hope of his Pasch are proclaimed and celebrated. Communities that want to share in this unity of order through the sacrament of order, even when this involves pain, express the desire for a communion in faith beyond their own boundaries.

10. The polemic is most ardently pursued in "The Abomination of the Secret Mass," *Luther's Works,* 36 (Philadelphia: Fortress, 1955): 314–23, but this needs to be read in conjunction with his early doctrine of the Lord's Supper and Testament given in the early work, "A Treatise on the New Testament, that is, the Mass," *Luther's Works,* 35: 75–112.

11. Mary Collins, "The Public Language of Ministry," *Worship: Renewal and Practice* (Washington, D.C.: The Pastoral Press, 1987): 137–73.

12. As I have shown elsewhere, the distinction is actually an adapted use of a distinction made by the Council of Trent in the treatment of celebrations in which only the priest takes communion. See David N. Power, *The Sacrifice We Offer: The Tridentine Dogma and its Reinterpretation* (New York: Crossroad, 1987): 25.

13. See Julia Kristeva, "From Symbol to Sign," and "Semiotics: A Critical Science and/or a Critique of Science," in *The Kristeva Reader,* ed. Tori Moi (New York: Columbia University Press, 1986): 34–88.

14. John Paul II, "Apostolic Letter on Ordination and Women," *Origins* 24/4 (1994): 49–52.

15. See David N. Power, "Representing Christ in Community and Sacrament," in *Being a Priest Today*, ed. Donald J. Goergen (Collegeville: The Liturgical Press, 1992): 97–123.

16. For some tentative moves on this question, see the letter of the USA Bishops, "Guidelines for Celebration of Sacraments with Persons with Disabilities," *Origins* 25/7 (1995): 105–110.

17. The factual reality of any Christian body requires expression in the sacramental action. Thus sufferers from AIDS ought to be sacramentally an integral part of a Christian community, not marginal to it; so should survivors of sexual or marital abuse. The hungry and the poor, it seems, are rarely offered the chair of the bishop or presider.

18. This is now remarked chiefly in relation to African, Asian and Indian cultures, whose peoples have been evangelized within the millennium drawing to a close. However, recent interest in Celtic Christianity notes how it and its centering in nature were suppressed around the advent of this same millennium. Among other works on the presence of the cosmic in this tradition, see Noel Dermot O'Donoghue, *The Mountain Behind the Mountain; Aspects of the Celtic Tradition* (Edinburgh: T & T Clark Ltd., 1993).

19. This is not developed in this essay, but encounter with other religious traditions is bound to have an effect on the theology and practice of the eucharist.

Ritual Studies and the Eucharist
Paying Attention to Performance

MARGARET MARY KELLEHER, OSU

Evidence of one way that the field of liturgical studies has expanded in the past 25 years is the work on ritual studies and the eucharist. During the early 1970s, some liturgical scholars in this country began to give serious attention to the study of ritual as they sought to learn more about the nature and dynamics of liturgy.[1] Mary Collins has been a major figure among those responsible for promoting an interdisciplinary approach to the study of liturgy that incorporates ritual theory.[2] I have her to thank for suggesting, some years ago, that I turn to ritual theory to see if there were resources there to answer some of my questions about liturgy.

I plan to address three questions here: Why attend to liturgical performance,in particular, the performance of the eucharist? To what does one attend? And what are some observations and questions that arise when one pays attention to the church performing the eucharist?

Performance as a Liturgical Source

Why pay attention to liturgical performance? My answer is that it is called for by the very nature of liturgy as action — to be more specific, as ecclesial action. We are all familiar with those statements in *The Constitution on the Sacred Liturgy* that identify liturgy as an action of Christ the priest and of his body, the church (7), that present liturgy as the place where the mystery of Christ and the real nature of the true church are manifest (2), and that stress the point that liturgical services are celebrations of the church (26). While noting the ecclesial nature of the liturgy, Vatican II also gave a definite primacy to the eucharist as the liturgical event in which the church is realized, and recognized that this happens in local communities.[3]

Statements such as these indicate that, by its very nature, liturgy is performative. It exists only in performance. We have many liturgical books, ancient and new, that are rich resources for liturgical studies; but liturgical texts do not become liturgy until they are performed by concrete local assemblies. If this is so, then surely liturgical performance is a significant source of data for liturgical studies.

There is a well-known principle that the church makes the eucharist and the eucharist makes the church.[4] Both the church and the eucharist are in transition as we move toward the third millennium. Conciliar statements such as those I mentioned above give evidence of a recovery of an ancient tradition that the *ecclesia,* the Christian community, is the subject of liturgical action.[5] The church is still in the process of receiving that teaching, and local assemblies all over the world are negotiating their identity as acting subjects of the eucharist. This process of discovery is related to the provocative claim made some years ago by Karl Rahner that, at Vatican II, the church took the first step toward realizing itself as a world church, "one which begins to act through the reciprocal influence exercised by all its components."[6] We are still negotiating our passage toward that reality. What kind of eucharist does a world church make?

Times of transition are somewhat dangerous because those in transition are neither here nor there. They are in liminality.[7] There is a certain quality of danger to such times, and there is the potential for creativity. If the church is being constituted in its celebrations of the eucharist, how can we ignore liturgical performance as a source for theological reflection about what we are becoming? It is in celebrations of the eucharist, as well as in other rituals, that we will find the church performing those beliefs, memories, hopes and values that are being carried into the twenty-first century. Here we have a significant source for discovering how the church's living tradition is being shaped and handed on.

page 53

Those in liturgical studies who have made the move to incorporate liturgical performance as a source of data are part of a trend that cuts across many disciplines. In a survey of theories of performance, Lawrence Sullivan identifies linguistics, cultural anthropology, sociology, performing arts, ethnomedicine, comparative law, social psychology, ethnomusicology and religious studies among the fields of study which have representatives exploring the nature of performance.[8] A number of scholars within these disciplines are interested in the role of performance in constituting knowledge and identity, and in my own work I have suggested that liturgy is a form of ecclesial ritual praxis in which the church itself is mediated.[9]

Ritual is often a subject of study for those who attend to performance, action, practice or praxis.[10] The field of ritual studies provides a rich resource for those liturgical scholars who become convinced of the need to include liturgical performance as a source of data for their work.

What happens when one incorporates ideas and methods from ritual studies into one's study of the eucharist? To what does one attend? What kinds of questions does one ask? Of course that depends on one's operative definition of ritual, and there are many possibilities here, not all of which are compatible. One who follows Roy Rappaport in defining ritual as "the performance of more or less invariant sequences of formal acts and utterances not encoded by the performers"[11] will have a very different methodological perspective from one who has been influenced by Ronald Grimes's interest in studying the exercise of ritual creativity in what he calls the process of "ritualizing" or "emerging ritual."[12] A third approach, which takes something of a middle ground between these two while capturing something of the dynamic, personal, social and constitutive nature of ritual, is that of Roland Delattre. He defines ritual as "those carefully rehearsed symbolic motions and gestures through which we regularly go, in which we articulate the felt shape and rhythm of our own humanity and of reality as we experience it, and by means of which we negotiate the terms or conditions for our presence among, and our participation in, the plurality of realities through which our humanity makes its passage."[13] In her book *Ritual Theory, Ritual Practice* Catherine Bell moves away from offering a definition of ritual as such and uses aspects of practice theory to develop a notion of ritualization as "a strategic way of acting in specific social situations."[14]

Like Grimes and others, I have never found Victor Turner's definition of ritual as "prescribed formal behavior for occasions not given over to technological routine, having reference to beliefs in mystical beings or powers"[15] adequate to cover all that he had to say about ritual in his writings. Turner himself recognized the inadequacies of his definition, noting that it was a "flat description" of ritual action which gives no indication of what the ritual might mean to those who enact it, or of a ritual's capacity to be transformative, spontaneous and responsive to a contemporary situation.[16] However, he continued to find his definition useful because he liked "to think of ritual essentially as *performance, enactment,* not primarily as rules or rubrics."[17] While I have not made use of his definition, my own understanding of ritual as social, symbolic and processual action in which meanings and values can be communicated, created and transformed is largely based on Turner's work.[18] Anyone who brings such an understanding of ritual to the study of liturgy must attend to ritual fields and to ritual bodies performing in those fields. Let me elaborate.

Moving into the Ritual Field

When one decides to study liturgical performance, one has to leave the study *page 55* and the library for a while and go into the field. The notion of ritual field is complex and expansive in both a synchronic and diachronic fashion. One goes to study liturgical performance in a particular community, such as a parish or university. In Turner's terminology, one has entered the "action-field context" of a ritual.[19] He emphasizes the significance of this context, for it is here that some of the many meanings associated with a ritual symbol will become apparent. Some of these may be innovations with respect to those meanings that are found in official sources.

There are so many elements included within a field that it can be likened to an ecosystem. A ritual has significance only as part of a broader field, and each element of a ritual becomes significant because of its relationship with other elements in that field. Among the elements included in the action-field context of any ritual are the following:

—the structure of the group that is performing the ritual
—its principles of organization and relationships
—the divisions and alliances operative within the group
at present and in its past.[20]

These can be identified as the social dimensions of the field. The spatial limits of the ritual field are also significant, for they play a role in shaping the composition of the ritual assembly.[21] The temporal limits and history of the social field call for attention because ritual symbols are connected with the life of a group and are affected by major events that have taken place within this life. In other words, ritual symbols have a "social history."[22] The symbols of bread, wine, cup and table that are central in the eucharist carry many meanings that are the outcome of centuries of eucharistic celebrations.

In addition to the social, spatial and temporal elements that constitute a ritual's field of action, the ritual's relationship with other rituals must also be considered. Although each ritual is a system of meanings in itself, it is only one part of a whole system of rituals performed by a group and receives additional meaning from its relationship with those rituals.[23] Following this, a study of the eucharist in any particular field might well include some effort to reflect on celebrations of the eucharist within the context of other rituals performed by the assemblies being studied. This might include giving some attention to the ritual performance of other sacraments, funerals, public devotions and so on.

The notion of field I have been discussing is a very broad one that provides the context within which a particular ritual is actually performed by an assembly. In such a performance, people, objects, gestures, words, sounds and actions all interact within an immediate ritual field defined by the kind of place and space in which a ritual occurs.[24] For example, one might be focusing a study on the liturgy of the eucharist within Sunday Mass as celebrated by a particular assembly. Within the immediate field defined by that segment of the ritual are such elements as persons, bread, wine, chalice, altar, prayers prayed, music played, songs sung, actions of giving and receiving and movement of persons in relation to the altar and one another; but the shape of the field of an assembly celebrating in a Gothic cathedral will differ radically from that of an assembly celebrating in a small chapel of contemporary design, and that difference will affect whatever meanings are mediated in the performance.

Individual elements as well as relationships established within an immediate field can provide significant data for exploring the visions of church and eucharist that are being publicly mediated in the celebrations of any assembly. Of course that data has to be placed in dialogue with data gathered from studying the broader ritual field, and the ensuing task of interpretation takes one back to the study. It is a task filled with complexity, and I have written about it elsewhere.[25]

Ritual Bodies in the Field

I hope it has become evident that when one goes into the field to study the *page 57* eucharist, one has to pay attention to the ritual body performing the liturgy. It is a body of bodies, and the body performing in each ritual field is involved in negotiating its identity as the body of Christ realized in this particular place. Just imagine some of the diversity of assemblies, of ritual bodies gathering any Sunday throughout the world to perform the eucharist. There are assemblies gathering in poor urban parishes, in cathedrals, in small rural villages, in university chapels, in suburban churches. The ritual body may be rather homogeneous in terms of ethnic and economic background or it may be filled with great diversity. In each one, something of the church's beliefs, memories, hopes and vision is being set out, and the church is being realized.

In his video *The Dancing Church*, Tom Kane has given us some wonderful illustrations of the variety of ritual bodies performing liturgy in several countries of Africa.[26] Bodily movement is central to the making of the eucharist in these local churches, and dance is clearly a mode of ritual prayer. Anyone wanting to study the theology of the eucharist operative in these churches would have to give careful attention to their ritual performance and, perhaps, reflect critically on some of the public meanings that are being mediated.[27] In watching the diversity of patterns of movement from place to place in this film, one begins to get a sense of the role of dance as a contributing factor in the complex process of mediating a world church. Elochukwu Uzukwu argues that the gestures, rhythms, sounds and bodily movements that are integral to dance in African liturgy mediate a vision of the universe for local communities and serve as carriers of the memory of Jesus.[28]

Paying attention to the body has been characteristic of the work of many of those engaged in the study of ritual. Ronald Grimes has argued that "the roots of ritual are inescapably biological and natural"[29] and has identified bodily gestures and postures as "the smallest units of action to which a ritologist assigns meaning."[30] In fact, he claims that ritual studies "begins by attending to gesture and posture, the actual comportment of the body in interaction."[31] Victor Turner gave extensive attention to human bodies in his studies of Ndembu ritual and argued that the human organism and its crucial experiences, rather than society, "are the *fons et origo* of all classifications."[32] In his theory about how ritual symbols operate, the biological referents of multivocal symbols have a crucial role to play and, toward the end of his life, Turner found some support for this hypothesis in the work of some neurobiologists.[33] In my own theory of liturgy as a form of ecclesial ritual praxis, I identify it as an example of incarnate meaning.[34]

Since the ritual body is a body of bodies, there are both individual and social dimensions of the body that call for attention. Those who participate in the rituals of a social body over a period of time acquire what Catherine Bell calls "ritual mastery," a term she uses "to designate a practical mastery of the schemes of ritualization as an embodied knowing, as the sense of ritual seen in its exercise."[35] Such ritual mastery gives those who possess it an ability to play significant roles in the shaping of a culture. Since ritual plays a crucial role in the articulation of personal and corporate identity, Roland Delattre notes how important it is in situations of cultural pluralism that individuals and communities acquire ritual competence, that they develop a variety of ritual capacities and the resourcefulness to make use of them.[36] Those who do this often engage in "ritualizing": creating rites in response to particular situations. As Grimes notes, ritualizing happens on the margins and is often not given social support. Because of this, it can sometimes be an interesting source of embodied criticism.[37]

At the beginning of this essay, I mentioned that both the church and the eucharist are in transition as we move into the third millennium. As ecclesial bodies throughout the world negotiate their passage toward becoming active subjects of the liturgy in a world church, they will be relying on

RITUAL STUDIES AND THE EUCHARIST

their ritual competence and resourcefulness to help them through the transition. The ritual performances of the eucharist by such bodies provide a rich resource of data for studying the process of negotiation and for discovering what beliefs, memories, hopes and relationships are being articulated as constitutive for ecclesial identity. Paying attention to the ritual body in this case is extremely important, since the body being mediated is the body of Christ.

page 59

Observations and Questions

What does one learn, and what new questions does one ask when one begins to pay attention to performance, in particular, the performance of the eucharist? Since there are many observations that can be made and numerous questions that arise, I will mention only a few. One of the first things that struck me, and continues to intrigue me, is the significant role ritual subjects play in shaping whatever meanings are made public in the performance. I suspect we all have witnessed how the same liturgical book used in different assemblies can result in very different ritual performances. Some of this has to do with choices made by persons involved in liturgical ministries. It also has something to do with the composition of the assembly and the quality of presence within the ritual body. We need to learn how to pay better attention to these factors and to movement, sound, gesture and music.

A second observation I want to make is that going into the field and acting as a participating observer in various ritual bodies has convinced me that the boundaries of our theologies of the eucharist have to be expansive enough to include questions concerning ecclesiology, christology, pneumatology, the Trinity and theological anthropology. I see the category of *koinonia,* or communion, as one that may be particularly fruitful here, but it must be developed in a way that takes actual assemblies into consideration. How can we incorporate the notion of the ritual body more fully into theological discussions of the making of the eucharist and the mediation of communion?

Exploring such a question calls for an interdisciplinary approach that will stretch the boundaries of our theology even further.

The diversity of ritual bodies performing the eucharist in a great variety of fields suggests many possibilities for study. There are bodies who gather in parishes on Sundays but cannot fully celebrate the eucharist because they are deprived of an ordained minister. Their ritual performance may consist of a service of the word, prayers and reception of communion. There are bodies of women who gather in homes or other settings and celebrate what they believe to be the eucharist, although here too, no ordained minister presides. Then there are the countless assemblies who gather weekly and celebrate the eucharist according to an approved liturgical book and with an ordained presbyter presiding. While I would expect a good bit of ritualizing to take place in the gatherings of women, I would not be surprised to find a certain amount of creative resourcefulness at work in the ritual activity of the assemblies in parishes either. If the church and eucharist are mutually constitutive, extended case studies of the ritual performance of all kinds of assemblies should provide plenty of data for exploring what understandings of eucharist, church and ministry are being publicly mediated in these performances.

When one studies liturgical performance, one becomes more aware of the ambiguity of ritual symbols. Symbols that are central in a community's tradition carry many meanings, and only some of the potential meanings are usually made available in any ritual performance. Sometimes the ritual performance can suggest a new and even contradictory meaning for a symbol. For example, the symbol of the chalice or the cup, which is so central to the eucharist, can become a symbol of privilege and distinction in the body rather than a symbol of communion because of restrictions placed on its availability to the assembly in certain ritual performances.[38]

When one studies liturgical performance within the context of a ritual system and looks at an assembly's rituals in relation to one another, one sometimes detects conflicting messages being set out for the ritual body.

I have seen this in my own studies of Christian initiation.[39] The tradition handed on in the New Testament and in our rituals of baptism teaches us that all who are baptized are made members of Christ, brought into the same body through the gift of the Spirit. All share in the same life and are in mutual communion; yet when some ritual bodies gather to celebrate the eucharist, the sacrament of ecclesial identity, there is a noticeable absence of female bodies preaching or leading assemblies in their eucharistic prayer at the table. Are our performances of the eucharist at times a countersign to our performances of baptism? Is the theology of communion performed in our eucharistic assemblies adequate to the theology which is set out in baptism?

page 61

Conclusion

In this paper I have asked you to imagine ritual fields and ritual bodies, and as I close, I suggest still another image: There is a river running through each of those many fields and through the bodies in each field. Think of it as the river of the waters of life (Revelations 22:1). Think of it as the eucharistic tradition. Think of it in Jean Corbon's words as the "wellspring of worship," the ultimate source of liturgy.[40] When those bodies in the field gather to celebrate the eucharist, they gather at this river.

In one of his essays, Victor Turner likened the rules and rubrics associated with ritual to banks that serve as a frame for a river.[41] The rules frame the ritual performance, but the flow of action and interaction within that performance may generate new insights and even new symbols and meanings that may be incorporated into subsequent performances. As a result, traditional framings may have to be reframed; in other words, the river seeks and finds new banks. As the church negotiates its passage into the third millennium and into becoming a world church, I think we need to pay more attention to our ritual performances in the field and at the river. We need to see if new banks are being sought, and we need to ask what our ritual bodies are contributing to the river's flow.

MARGARET MARY KELLEHER, OSU

Endnotes

1. For an introduction to some approaches and issues within the field of ritual studies, see *Liturgy Digest* 1:1 (1993).

2. See Mary Collins, OSB, *Worship: Renewal to Practice* (Washington, D.C.: The Pastoral Press, 1987) for several essays which incorporate ritual theory.

3. See, for example, *Sacrosanctum concilium* 2, 41, 42 and *Lumen gentium* 26. English translation by the International Commission on English in the Liturgy(ICEL), in *Documents on the Liturgy: 1963–1979 Conciliar, Papal, and Curial Texts* (Collegeville: Liturgical Press, 1982).

4. For the statement of this principle, see Henri de Lubac, *Méditation sur l'Église* (Paris: Éditions Montaigne, 1953): 113.

5. Yves M. J. Congar made this claim in "L'Ecclesia ou communauté chrétienne, sujet intégral de l'action liturgique," in *La Liturgie après Vatican II*, ed. J. P. Jossua and Y. Congar (Paris: Cerf 1967): 241.

6. Karl Rahner, "Towards a Fundamental Theological Interpretation of Vatican II," *Theological Studies* 40 (1979): 717.

7. Victor Turner developed Arnold Van Gennep's notion of the liminal in many of his works. See, for example, "Process, System, and Symbol: A New Anthropological Synthesis," *Daedalus* 106:3 (1977): 67–69.

8. Lawrence E. Sullivan, "Sound and Senses: Toward a Hermeneutics of Performance," *History of Religions* 26 (1986–87): 5–14.

9. See Margaret Mary Kelleher, "Liturgy: An Ecclesial Act of Meaning," *Worship* 59 (1985): 482–97.

10. See Sherry Ortner, "Theory in Anthropology Since the Sixties," *Comparative Studies in Society and History* 26 (1984): 144–57, for a discussion of the growing interest in the analysis of practice, praxis, action, interaction, activity, experience and performance which emerged in the 1980s. She, like Sullivan, notes the diversity of disciplines involved in the movement.

11. Roy A. Rappaport, "Ritual, Time, and Eternity," *Zygon* 27:1 (1992): 5.

12. See Ronald L. Grimes, "Reinventing Ritual," *Soundings* 75:1 (1992): 21–41.

13. Roland A. Delattre, "Ritual Resourcefulness and Cultural Pluralism," *Soundings* 61 (1978): 282.

14. Catherine Bell, *Ritual Theory, Ritual Practice* (New York: Oxford University Press, 1992): 67.

15. Victor Turner, *The Forest of Symbols: Aspects of Ndembu Ritual* (Ithaca: Cornell University Press, 1967): 19.

16. Victor Turner, "Encounter with Freud: The Making of a Comparative Symbologist," in *The Making of Psychological Anthropology*, ed. George D. Spindler (Berkeley: University of California Press, 1978): 560.

17. Victor Turner, "Social Dramas and Stories About Them" in *From Ritual to Theatre: The Human Seriousness of Play* (New York: PAJ Publications 1982): 79.

18. See Kelleher, "Liturgy: An Ecclesial Act," pp. 488–91, and Margaret Mary Kelleher, "Liturgical Theology: A Task and a Method," *Worship* 62 (1988): 11–12.

19. Turner, *The Forest,* p. 43.

20. Ibid., 47.

21. Ibid., 262–64.

22. Victor Turner and Edith Turner, *Image and Pilgrimage in Christian Culture: Anthropological Perspectives* (New York: Columbia University Press, 1978): 146.

23. Turner, *The Forest,* p. 46.

24. Ronald Grimes offers a variety of questions for "Mapping the Field of Ritual" in *Beginnings in Ritual Studies,* rev. ed. (Columbia: University of South Carolina Press, 1995): 24–39.

25. Margaret Mary Kelleher, "Hermeneutics in the Study of Liturgical Performance," *Worship* 67 (1993): 292–318.

26. Thomas A. Kane, *The Dancing Church: Video Impressions of the Church in Africa* (New York: Paulist Press 1992), 58 minutes. For a review of the video, see R. Kevin Seasoltz, "*The Dancing Church:* An Appreciation," *Worship* 67 (1993): 253–61.

27. Seasoltz notes the emphasis given to the text of institution within the eucharistic prayer and offers some critical reflections. See pages 260–61.

28. Elochukwu E. Uzukwu, "Body and Memory in African Liturgy," in *Liturgy and the Body,* Concilium 3, ed. Louis-Marie Chauvet and Francois Kabasele Lumbala (Orbis: Maryknoll, 1995): 72–73.

29. Ronald L. Grimes, "Modes of Ritual Sensibility," in *Beginnings,* p. 44.

30. Ronald L. Grimes, "Sitting and Eating," in *Beginnings,* p. 90.

31. Ibid., 91.

32. Turner, *Forest,* p. 90.

33. Victor Turner, "Body, Brain, and Culture," in *On the Edge of the Bush: Anthropology as Experience,* ed. Edith L. B. Turner (Tucson: The University of Arizona Press, 1985): 270–71.

34. See Kelleher, "Liturgy: An Ecclesial Act," *Worship* 62 (1988): 492.

35. Bell, *Ritual Theory, Ritual Practice,* p. 107.

36. See Delattre, "Ritual Resourcefulness," pp. 281–82.

37. See Ronald L. Grimes, "Emerging Ritual," *Reading, Writing, and Ritualizing: Ritual in Fictive, Liturgical, and Public Places* (Washington, D.C.: The Pastoral Press, 1993): 23–26.

38. See Margaret Mary Kelleher, "The Communion Rite: A Study of Roman Catholic Liturgical Performance," *Journal of Ritual Studies* 5 (1991): 110–17.

page 63

MARGARET MARY KELLEHER, osu

39. See Margaret Mary Kelleher, "Liturgy as a Source for Sacramental Theology," *Questions Liturgiques* 72 (1991): 33–35.

40. See Jean Corbon, *The Wellspring of Worship,* trans. Matthew J. O'Connell (Mahwah: Paulist Press, 1988).

41. Turner, "Social Dramas," p. 79.

The Critical Task
of Liturgical Theology
Prospects and Proposals

KEVIN W. IRWIN

My main focus in studying, teaching and writing about the liturgy has been the area of liturgical theology. By liturgical theology I mean appreciating the theological depth and breadth of the liturgy as well as probing the spiritual and ethical implications of celebrating liturgy in terms of appreciating how the liturgy forms us and informs our life values and actions. The maxim for this enterprise is lex orandi, lex credendi: *"The law of prayer grounds the law of belief."* Sounds simple? Not for very long!

Because all liturgy has a history, its very evolution reflects variety and pluriformity in ritual and in theology. Different liturgical forms and texts "say" different things. Liturgy was, and always is, inculturated, and with that inculturation comes a dynamic *orthopraxis* and its complement, *orthodoxy*. Thus the church's liturgy — even the present reformed liturgy — must be seen in relation to its historical evolution, with one of the tasks of liturgical theology being that of evaluating what the liturgy might say and do in light of our theological and liturgical tradition. In a sense, no liturgical rite is ever totally "right" — hence the phrase "the critical task" of liturgical theology.[1] Even the often extolled Tridentine Missal stood in need of "correction" (to quote Paul VI).[2]

It is frequently stated that the post–Vatican II liturgical reform consists of two intrinsically related phases: (1) the restoration of the "classical" (pre-eighth-century) Roman practice, and then (2) the adaptation of these rather sober and direct rites to the variety of local, contemporary cultures. I would argue, therefore, that the present reformed liturgy stands in need of scrutiny as well as constructive proposals for its ongoing implementation.[3] In that process, both *orandi* and *credendi* play significant, complementary roles.

My concern here is with a critical assessment of the Roman Missal as it presently exists (and of parts of the proposed second edition of the sacramentary in English) in light of both the history and theology of Western liturgy and contemporary need. For the most part, I shall be concerned with some aspects of the *structure and texts* of the present Roman eucharistic rite and some proposals for the forthcoming second vernacular English edition. I will rely on the classic phrase *lex orandi, lex credendi* but will also emphasize that we are dealing with *enacted rites,* not just texts, and with the ethical implications of the eucharist, not just ritual events.[4] Thus we must be attentive to the enacted rites — *lex agendi* — as the place where we experience liturgy's *lex orandi* and be aware that enacted rites lead to *shaping values* among worshipers that are congruent with the liturgy and to *living life* in accord with what we celebrate — *lex vivendi.*

It seems to me that the present Roman eucharistic rite has appropriately reestablished the primacy of *proclamation* of both the Word and the eucharistic prayer and the assembly's participation through listening, posture and sung response.[5] In what follows I will only make mention of some parts of the church's traditional eucharistic *orandi* to supplement what we now have. However, it also seems to me that there are structural problems with what might be termed the "transition rites" within the eucharist, namely the *opening rites*, the *presentation of the gifts* and the *rites of communion*. The agenda *page 67* at the time of the revision was to remove the extraneous elements that came to be added to these rites when the Roman rite was accepted in Gaul. This has occurred to a large extent,[6] but problems remain.

First, the "transition rites" involve the *movement* and *involvement* of the assembly—factors ignored in the Tridentine liturgy and poorly established in the rubrical directives for the enactment of the present reformed rites. Can one not say that the *lex agendi* of the assembly has been all but ignored in the present Missal? The repeated goal from the *Constitution on the Sacred Liturgy* of Vatican II of "full, conscious and active participation" by the assembly in the liturgy is not sustained in the way the eucharistic rite describes exactly what the assembly should do at the eucharist. Where the present sacramentary does indicate the postures of the assembly, those directions are not always the most fortuitous, namely, kneeling for the major portion of the eucharistic prayer; standing would seem the most logical, traditional and desirable choice today.[7]

Second, real questions can be asked about the adequacy of the way the Roman Missal describes the actions that occur in these transition rites and how it describes their theological meaning (more to follow).

Third, the present Roman liturgy lacks the *primalness* (for want of a better term) of even the former rite. The traditions of ember and rogation days, specific aspects of this primal rootedness of the eucharist, have regrettably gone by the boards. Even at the Easter Vigil, when the primal elements of earth, air, fire and water receive emphasis, the appropriate restoration of adult initiation at Easter tends to eclipse these fundamental aspects of rite both experientially and theologically.

Fourth, the tradition of Jewish and Christian prayer is to call on God "creator and redeemer." My assessment is that we do little justice either to naming God as creator or to the theology of creation used in the liturgy to express God's largesse and sustaining love.

page 68

Fifth, the present eucharistic liturgy pays scant attention to *eschatology*, save for its (perhaps over-) emphasis on intercession. This is to say that references to how the present eucharistic liturgy leads to the eschatological banquet are scarce, aside from the invitation to communion and the prayer after the rite of water blessing and sprinkling on Sundays.[8]

These five principal concerns ground what now follows about the liturgy of the Eucharist.[9]

1. Entrance Rites

Many others have written of the "cluttered vestibule" of the Order of Mass.[10] The present ICEL proposals to deal with this (at least moderately confusing) ritual action for the revision of the Roman Missal seem quite appropriate and desirable.[11] I do not intend to rehearse these valuable studies and proposals except to say that in them, the helpful prayer that concludes the sprinkling rite —

> May almighty God cleanse us of our sins
> and through the celebration of this eucharist
> make us worthy to sit
> at the table of the kingdom forever.
> Amen.

will likely become an option for the absolution as part of the penitential rites. This is a decided advantage. Since there are so few references to eschatology in the eucharistic liturgy, I would hope that this prayer would be used more regularly in celebration.

I want to raise the question of what is the first musical participation of the assembly—their *agendi* in the liturgy's *orandi*—namely the "entrance song." I have written elsewhere that I judge the use of the metrical hymn to be inappropriate as part of the eucharistic entrance rite[12] and that the singing of antiphons and psalm verses is most appropriate to accompanying the entrance procession. My concern here is to argue that for ritual, pedagogical and spiritual reasons, we ought to use the same translation for the psalms used in the eucharist and in the Liturgy of the Hours. Presently we use translations for antiphons in the Order of Mass that are different from those of the responsorial psalm in the liturgy of the word, both of which are different from the New American Bible psalter translation for the responsorial psalms at the eucharist and the Grail psalter (most commonly) used at Hours. My liturgical and pastoral concern is that the use of these different translations has removed the psalter from usefulness as the church's prayerbook—both in liturgical gatherings and in domestic prayer. The recent publication of the ICEL psalter goes a long way toward giving us a text that is usable for liturgy and for other prayer. My hope is that familiarity with the translation of the psalms can only help facilitate participation in liturgy, enrich prayer engaged in outside the liturgy and help communities of faith deepen their familiarity both with the proclaimed scriptures that are constitutive of the reformed liturgy and with the Bible itself as the heart of personal prayer and guide for Christian spirituality. In fact, the legitimate call for *lament* in eucharistic euchology,[13] specifically the eucharistic prayer, has its origin in the lament psalms themselves; hence the more frequent use of all the psalms in a familiar translation is an urgent need.

My second concern with the entrance rites concerns the opening prayer—*orandi/credendi*. Historical scholarship discloses a variety of answers to the question, "What is it?" Authors argue about whether this prayer concludes the entrance rites or refers to the scripture readings of the day, feast or season when the eucharist is celebrated.[14] Added to this is the present Western practice of frequently using the same collect at Mass and at the

page 69

Liturgy of the Hours, whose liturgies are of different origin and have different theologies. One must be careful, therefore, at being too certain that we know the nature and function of this prayer.

My particular difficulty concerns whether the prayer is too generic on the one hand or too specific on the other. Instead of being a rather generic prayer that can be used in a number of places in the liturgy, could one not argue that the opening prayer of the eucharist should articulate in some fashion the fact that, and why, the assembly has gathered for this eucharist (as opposed to gathering for the Hours)?

The question of specificity is a bit more dicey. As you well know, the present second edition of the Italian sacramentary for Sundays contains a translation of the Roman Missal's opening prayer and three additional original compositions to coincide with the three cycles of the Sunday lectionary. The present proposals for the second edition of the English sacramentary follow this same format. I welcome this variety in euchology. However, my question concerns whether regular recourse to the prayers composed to reflect the readings will make the collect a rather didactic moment in the eucharistic liturgy, especially if the introduction to the day's liturgy also refers to the day's scriptures. It is at least arguable that the intrinsic connection of word and table — so that these are seen to be one act of worship (as is repeatedly stated in every magisterial document since Vatican II) — could be mitigated when the opening prayer refers exclusively to our praying texts that refer specifically to the day's scriptures.

2. Presentation of the Gifts

Once again we are indebted to liturgical scholars and theologians for rich insight into the present revision of the rites for presenting the gifts and preparing the altar for the eucharistic prayer.[15] My concern here is with the sacramentality of creation, the theology of stewardship and the theological meaning of any prayers accompanying these rites, including the prayer over the gifts.

As we face the third millennium, it would seem opportune to emphasize some characteristic tenets of Roman Catholic belief. A particularly strong suit in Catholic theology, belief and practice is *sacramentality,* which means that we discover the divine in the human and that the world as we know it is the locus of divine revelation. In fact, the world and all creation is the reflection of God, who made them "good." Liturgy capitalizes on this theology by using the goods of this earth in our communal act of worship;[16] hence in the eucharist, we use the gifts of creation and the gift of human productivity to manufacture the central symbols of bread and wine.[17] The church's *lex agendi* repeatedly articulates this notion of sacramentality in the celebration of eucharist.

page 71

This is closely related, in my view, to *stewardship.* If, in fact, this notion includes "time, talent and treasure," then I think that a classical locus for the liturgy's articulation of offering time and talent is in the rites of presenting bread and wine for the celebration of the eucharist. The phrase "no work, no Mass" reveals layers of meaning and important insight. It seems to me that the controversy this past decade-and-a-half over ensuring that eucharistic breads are unleavened has had the unfortunate effect of diminishing any significant involvement of the community in preparing its own eucharistic bread and wine. That creativity and labor—focused on the true *sacramentality* of the gifts presented—is in need of retrieval.

Liturgical tradition also supports the intrinsic connection between presenting bread and wine for the eucharist with collecting gifts to be shared with the poor and needy of the community.[18] The issue I want to raise concerns the extent to which what is conventionally called the "offertory collection" of money is catechized about and perceived as an act of communal self-transcendence and sharing from our substance for the poor and needy. (Or is it understood as the means whereby parishes make their weekly budget commitments for staff and programs, especially in these days of cost-cutting and down- or "right"-sizing?) These latter are requisite demands, but concern for the poor, the needy and the marginalized—not just the mainstream—is part of our liturgical and theological tradition when presenting gifts at the eucharist.

Classically, the church's eucharistic *lex vivendi* reflected in its *lex orandi* was collecting gifts for the poor and distributing to those in need. In an era when we have restored the permanent diaconate, can one not ask whether the church has become any more convinced of its own fundamental status at the eucharist as permanently diaconal, serving others and constitutionally self-transcending? In a time when the self is prized in our culture and individual self-awareness is paramount, ought not the presentation of the eucharistic gifts remind us that the real issue is not self-perservation, or even the communal preservation of the assembly, but the communal transformation and self-transcendence of the church to become ever more what it is as servants of God and servants of the wider world? Has the concomitance of liturgical reform and the demand for social justice in this century in American liturgical circles, chiefly from Virgil Michel on, now been irretrievably lost? The image in John 13 is washing feet, not balancing budgets; the image of the Lukan Jesus is table fellowship with outcasts, not with the well-born (as in Luke 15, for example).

The present texts that accompany placing the bread and wine on the altar certainly go a long way toward eliminating the semi-duplication of the Roman Canon in the Tridentine "offertory prayers." The texts are not without difficulties, however, as is evident in the body of literature critiquing them and the gestures used to place the gifts on the altar. I am inclined to agree with those who argue that to articulate "Blessed are you, Lord God of all creation . . ." at this point is inappropriate, because the blessing genre from which these prayers derive is constitutive of the eucharistic prayer genre. This is to say that the insertion of these prayers, which were to eliminate the thematic duplication of the canon and the former offertory prayers, in fact do the same thing and repeat a classic theme of the anaphora! Given the sacramental value of creation itself and the value placed on human ingenuity in producing these gifts, it would seem that a redrafting of these texts is in order—if, in fact, texts are retained here at all (a point that has been appropriately debated). Here, the *Lutheran Book of Worship* offers some helpful insight in the anthem "Let the Vineyards Be Fruitful."[19]

It seems to me that many of the prayers over the gifts are proleptic, which is to say that they anticipate the transformation of the gifts into Christ's body and blood, and petition for what results from that unique paschal sacrifice. In line with what I have just argued, it would seem appropriate that some of these prayers speak directly to the sacramentality of creation and express how these humble gifts of bread and wine reflect service, homage and honor to God the creator.

page 73

3. The Eucharistic Prayer

I noted earlier that a main contribution of the present reform of the eucharist has been the due reemphasis now given to the eucharistic prayer, the high point of the celebration (GIRM, 156). Efforts underway in the United States toward singing this prayer with the acclamations of the assembly are to be applauded and encouraged. What is of particular interest to me here in terms of structure is the way some contemporary debates ensue regarding additional prefaces and eucharistic prayers. From Trent to today we have evolved from a single Roman canon to eight additional prayers (as of now) with a decided structure (GIRM, 55).

My concern is with this defined structure, and my argument is that it need not be the only plan for a eucharistic prayer. It seems to me that in debates about the relative merits of additional eucharistic prayers composed in English for inclusion into the English Order of Mass (for example, the ICEL text for Eucharistic Prayer "A"), very often the post–Vatican II eucharistic prayer structure has been regarded as so normative as not to be changed in any way. One could legitimately argue that the eucharistic prayer structure in the Masses with children (with its inclusion of acclamations throughout and the placement of the memorial acclamation after the memorial prayer with children) could be used as structural justification for an alternative prayer structure to include, for example, a single rather than a double epiclesis, the memorial acclamation after the memorial prayer, and so on.

With regard to content, it elsewhere has been argued very effectively that our present anaphoras are limiting in the way they image God and the human condition.[20] If in fact the preface is the classical place where we praise the God of creation and redemption, it seems to me that the first of these attributes is in need of enhancement in our euchology. The present prefaces are christologically and soteriologically rich, but they are rather scant in terms of referring to God as *creator*, in praising God for the act of creating the world and humankind and in saving history before Christ (except for Eucharistic Prayer IV). At present, naming God as creator occurs in the fourth eucharistic prayer.[21] In light of both liturgical tradition and the evidence in the present sacramentary, it would seem most fitting if the prefaces were to name and to articulate more fully who the God of creation is and how creation itself praises and thanks the God who made it. Furthermore, this kind of euchological restoration could lead to widening the social justice concern of eucharistic participation toward stewardship for the earth, care for the environment and awareness of communal culpability in the ecological crisis today. Caring for this good earth is a requisite ethical consequence of sharing in the eucharist, even as this meal for the pilgrim church leads to a new heaven and a new earth.

4. Communion Rites

Robert Taft has insightfully written that "the greatest and most successful liturgical reform in Catholic history is surely the movement for the restoration of frequent communion."[22] It seems clear that at the time of the revision of the Order of Mass, the present phenomenon of frequent reception of the eucharist by such vast numbers under both species was unforeseen. The rites of communion, derived largely from the Tridentine Missal, need reexamination and revision in light of liturgical tradition in order to meet this pastoral need.[23] As we experience what is truly a chief Catholic element of the eucharist—its frequent celebration and our communal participation in the eucharistic species—we know only too well that the present reformed liturgy is willing, but the rubric is weak.

The centrality and symbolic meaning of the fraction rite has received significant and due attention in this country. The use of large plates and flagons to contain the eucharistic gifts and the common extension of the sung Lamb of God have facilitated this. I would simply urge that, as much as possible, these actions of the fraction rite take place in such a way that the assembly can see what is happening. This means that, in very large assemblies, the priest and deacon (or eucharistic minister) might remain at the altar and the other eucharistic ministers would engage in this rite at a side table so as not to obstruct the visual impact of the fraction and pouring at the altar. This would allow the symbolic actions to be truly central, with clarity of vision and focus at the altar.

page 75

The proposed translation of the present invitation to communion reads as follows:

Behold the Lamb of God,
who takes away the sin of the world.
Blessed are those called to the supper of the Lamb.

This is a most helpful rendering of Revelation, 19:4, whose eschatology here is happily sustained. It underscores the multivalent nature of this text as referring to the eucharist being celebrated here and now, and to the heavenly banquet—the fulfillment of all liturgy. The second proposed option is equally multivalent in stating that those who eat "the bread come down from heaven . . . will live forever" and whoever drinks the "cup of eternal life . . . will live forever."

With regard to the reception of communion specifically, it seems to me that the Tridentine rite was concerned with the validity of the eucharist that the community *attended;* hence the priest's communion was very important to that end. Our present rubrics require that the priest receive communion first, followed by the deacon. However, it would seem that, given the regular reception of most of the assembly at every eucharist, the priest's act of receiving could legitimately follow everyone else's reception of communion. After all, the present rubric states that if the deacon is to minister the eucharistic cup, "he is the last to drink from it" (GIRM, 137). What was formerly a rubric to ensure validity could easily (and should) be changed to a rubric of hospitality, with clergy and all eucharistic ministers receiving last.

During the distribution, more attention needs to be given to the song that accompanies the act of communion. This unique sign of ecclesial communion—of the body of Christ in the body of Christ, the eucharist—needs to be underscored with appropriate expressions from the psalms or other antiphonal prayer that accompanies the procession and the action of taking and eating/drinking.

In presenting the eucharistic bread and cup for communion, the retention of the phrase "the body/blood of Christ" is helpful because, left this way, the text can be appreciated in a multivalent way. This is to say that the eucharist is underscored as a sharing in the person of Christ and in the ecclesial Body of Christ. Even the seemingly slight addition "*this is* the body of Christ" could skew this multivalence into focusing on the species only, which in fact the rite does not do.

5. Domestic Prayer and Meals

In an address at the biannual Societas Liturgica meeting in Dublin (August 1995), Irmgad Pahl argued that the mystery of God is revealed in the eucharist through the genre of the common meal.[24] Theologically she is quite right, but experientially I raise the question of whether the custom of the family meal is becoming more and more scarce in America today. Is that term—family meal—itself not a mystery? Or, in the words of a very provocative article by Margaret Mackenzie, "Is the Family Meal Disappearing?"[25]

What I raise here is a profound cultural question catechetically, ritually and sacramentally. At the eucharist we receive divine gifts from what is human—*sub specie humanitatis;* but what is occurring in our contemporary culture to that staple of family sharing and bonding when meals are less and less frequently taken together and when fast food really means not prepared at home or shared at a common table? In a culture that places a premium on time to do lots of things, including work and leisure activities, I wonder what kind of adequate liturgical theology and spirituality can be articulated about the eucharist if its domestic predication—dining together—is absent.

page 77

The issue is not sumptuous banquets over simple foods or feasting over modest food intake. The issue is to sacramentalize and ritualize whatever the domestic church shares as daily food and drink at table. This ritualizing would include blessing the God of creation and redemption, partaking of what we have prepared for others out of reverence and service, the honor we show to each other when we are at table with them and the conversations we have to show support for, and real interest in, others. In a culture of "meals on wheels" and "fast food" for quick consumption, do we not have to examine the bad habits of quick ingestion of food which forsake family unity, social interchange and family ties? At a time when American culture prizes "prayer breakfasts" as evidence of religious sensibility and "power lunches" as evidence of how to influence people, a strong Catholic suit would be to probe the profoundly spiritual reality of dining together and the power of communion derived from meals taken in common, as well as the eucharistic communion of meals through, with and in Christ.

Conclusion

I began by suggesting that my main focus in liturgical studies has been on liturgical theology and liturgical spirituality. My concern here has been to heighten and deepen our awareness of both at the present moment, over thirty years after Vatican II and as we face a new millennium of church life, with the eucharist and sacramentality as strong suits for Roman Catholicism.

Hosts of meaning are still to be unearthed and probed. In the meantime, a final recommendation for reflection, discussion and enjoyment: Go to the "foreign language" section of the local video store and rent *Babette's Feast*. There may well be more liturgical theology in the film *Babette's Feast* than we ever dreamed![26]

Endnotes

1. See, Angelus Haussling, "Die kritische Funktion der Liturgiewissenschaft," in *Liturgie und Gesellschaft,* ed. Hans B. Meyer (Innsbruck: Tyrolia Verlag, 1970): 103–130.

2. Paul VI, Apostolic Constitution *Missale Romanum* (1969) quoted in *Documents on the Liturgy 1963–1979* (Collegeville: The Liturgical Press, 1982): n. 1358.

page 79

3. We are truly at a new moment of liturgical reform and ongoing renewal today because we are asking questions of the documents of the present revised liturgy—both General Instructions and the rites themselves—that were not envisioned when they were written. The most poignant example regarding the eucharist is that two decades after the publication of the new Missal, the Vatican issued the *Directory for Sunday Celebrations in the Absence of a Priest* to meet a pastoral challenge not envisioned and not addressed in any of the very recent post–Vatican II revised rites.

4. In my own work *Context and Text: Method in Liturgical Theology* (Collegeville: The Liturgical Press, 1994), I stress throughout *lex agendi,* meaning enacted rites, as the source for theological reflection, and *lex vivendi* as response in life to the liturgy we have celebrated.

5. I defer here to my colleagues Dr. McManus, for observations on the adequacy of the cycle of readings for the *Lectionary for Mass,* and Dr. Kelleher, for observations on how well ritual performance matches up to the rites as envisioned.

6. Interestingly, Bugnini (in *The Reform of the Liturgy 1948–1975,* trans. Matthew O'Connell [Collegeville: The Liturgical Press, 1990]: 339) asserts that at the outset of undertaking the revision of the Order of Mass, it was clear that "the opening rites, the offertory, the communion and the dismissal" were "in need of careful revision."

7. See John K. Leonard and Nathan D. Mitchell, *The Postures of the Assembly During the Eucharistic Prayer* (Chicago: Liturgy Training Publications, 1994).

8. Greater attention to the eschatological would, I think, appropriately ground the social justice concerns that have been legitimately emphasized in recent years. In the liturgy we meet the *eschatos* whose life, death, resurrection and anticipated second coming ground us here and now in attitude and conduct.

9. In what follows I shall be dealing with Sunday eucharist as normative. If time and space had permitted, I would have liked to address issues such as varied rites for weekdays as opposed to Sunday eucharist (see Anscar J. Chupungco, "Towards A Ferial Rite of Mass," *Ecclesia Orans* 10 [1993]: 11–32), the theological and liturgical value of concelebration of presbyters with diocesan bishop, and the rather problematic value of daily presbyteral concelebration in monastic and religious communities as well as seminaries and formation communities (see my own "On Monastic Priesthood," *American Benedictine Review* 41 [1990]: 225–62, and among others, Marcel Rooney "Eucharistic Concelebration, Twenty-Five Years of Development," *Ecclesia Orans* 6 [1989]: 117–29).

10. For a most helpful historical study of the evolution of these rites, and comments from the way the present rite was implemented as summarized in the Notre Dame Study on Parish Worship, see Mark Searle, *"Semper Reformanda:* The Opening and Closing Rites of the Mass," in *Shaping English Liturgy,* ed. Peter C. Finn and James M. Schellman (Washington: The Pastoral Press, 1990): 53–92. A more

pastoral treatment is in Ralph Keifer, "Our Cluttered Vestibule: The Unreformed Entrance Rite," *Worship* 48 (1974): 270–77. For the greeting of the assembly, see Thomas A. Krosnicki, "Grace and Peace: Greeting the Assembly," *Shaping English Liturgy,* pp. 93–106.

11. See *Second Progress Report on the Revision of the Roman Missal* (Washington: ICEL, 1990): Appendix, pp. 93–95.

page 80   12. See *Context and Text,* pp. 237–40.

13. I refer to the work of my colleague David N. Power in this regard in *The Eucharistic Mystery: Revitalizing the Tradition* (New York: Crossroad, 1992).

14. The first chapter of Kathleen Hughes's unpublished doctoral dissertation, "The Opening Prayers of 'The Sacramentary': A Structural Study of the Prayers of the Easter Cycle" (University of Notre Dame, 1981), provides a fine summary of these debates.

15. See, among others, Frederick R. McManus, "The Roman Order of Mass from 1964–1969: The Preparation of the Gifts," in *Shaping English Liturgy,* pp. 107–138.

16. See my own, "The Sacramentality of Creation and the Role of Creation in Liturgy and Sacrament," in *Preserving the Creation: Environmental Theology and Ethics,* ed. Kevin W. Irwin and Edmund D. Pellegrino (Washington: Georgetown University Press, 1994): 67–111.

17. See Philippe Rouillard, "From Human Meal to Christian Eucharist," in *Living Bread, Saving Cup: Readings on the Eucharist,* ed. R. Kevin Seasoltz (Collegeville: The Liturgical Press, 1982): 126–57.

18. See the helpful treatment by Edward J. Kilmartin, "The Sacrifice of Thanksgiving and Social Justice," in *Liturgy and Social Justice,* ed. Mark Searle (Collegeville: The Liturgical Press, 1980): 53–71.

19. The irony should not be lost: The Lutheran tradition, which has shunned any sacrificial overtones, offers insight for this part of the liturgy that has these overtones in the Catholic tradition!

20. See David N. Power, *The Eucharistic Mystery.*

21. That God acts to create is found in the Roman Canon (before the *per ipsum: semper bona creas . . .*) and in the fifth Sunday preface *(omnibus quae creasti).*

22. Robert Taft, "The Frequency of the Eucharist Throughout History," in *Can We Always Celebrate the Eucharist?* Concilium 152, ed. David Power and Mary Collins (Edinburgh: T. and T. Clark, 1982): 19.

23. Most helpful in the interim is certainly Gabe Huck, *The Communion Rite at Sunday Mass* (Chicago: Liturgy Training Publications, 1989).

24. See Irmgad Pahl, "The Paschal Mystery in its Central Meaning for the Shape of Christian Liturgy," *Studia Liturgical* 26 (1996): 16–38, and Willy Rordorf, "A Response to the Paper of Irmgad Pahl," pp. 39–48.

25. *Journal of Gastronomy* 7 (Winter/Spring, 1993): 35–45.

26. See the helpful work by the medical doctor Leon Kass, *The Hungry Soul: Eating and Perfecting Our Nature* (New York: Free Press, 1994).

In Persona Christi
at the Eucharist

GERARD AUSTIN, OP

My topic here is one that will continue to be analyzed
and studied as we enter the third millennium. A great deal
has already been written on this topic in recent years, and
extremely important in this work is the study of a Dominican
fellow graduate student of mine, Bernard Marliangeas.[1] In
our own country, Worship *magazine did a service by pub-*
lishing six Forum *columns on the issue of* in persona
Christi *between 1989 and 1993.[2] More recently, there has*
been a lively exchange on the topic between Dennis Ferrara
and Sara Butler in Theological Studies.[3] *These articles are*
most helpful, and both authors have promised to continue to
publish on the topic.

In my own opinion, the most helpful article in the literature is by David N. Power.[4] I would also recommend an interesting article by Australian theologian David Coffey.[5] This literature, and that still to come, will continue to assist us while we study the issue as we move into the third millennium. As with most theological questions, it is important to identify where the discussion begins, what its starting point is, for where we begin a discussion often influences its conclusion. I would like to avoid an immediate comparison of the ordained priest to Christ and would offer four possible starting points, four "frameworks," that might lead to richer theological conclusions.

The first framework is the important issue of "the proper subject of the liturgical action." During my own days as a doctoral student, I was taught this by Father Yves Congar, OP, and it caused me to undergo an ecclesiological somersault.[6] He taught us that the church, the Christian community, was the proper subject of the liturgical action. The Mass, he told us, is an *actio*. Whose action is it? As a good Dominican, he built a syllogism: The Mass is the action of Christ, but we are Christ through our baptism; therefore, the Mass is our action, too.

With this syllogism he echoed Augustine: "Let us rejoice and give thanks. We have not only become Christians, but Christ himself. . . . Stand in awe and rejoice: We have become Christ."[7] In the early church, the *alter Christus* was not the priest but the baptized woman or man.

Examination of the early church witnesses shows that those who presided over the life of the church also presided over the eucharist. Indeed, presidency of the eucharistic assembly was seen as a liturgical dimension of the overall pastoral charge of building up the church. Furthermore, even in their own actions as heads of the assembly, the presidents of the eucharist acted as members of the assembly, for—as the liturgical vocabulary of the first millennium shows—the whole community celebrated and the whole community offered the sacrifice along with the priest-celebrant. The eucharistic prayer was expressed in the first person plural. "We come to You, Father, in a spirit of thanksgiving." The "we" is both the gathered assembly and the universal church. Since the Carolingian period, the relation between the priest and the "we" has been weakened;[8] yet, as late as the twelfth century, we hear someone liked Blessed Guerricus of Igny saying, "The priest does not consecrate alone, but the entire assembly of the faithful consecrate and sacrifice with him."[9]

page 83

This is a most crucial insight and one which I fear is lost in most popular thinking today. It is an insight that frames or contextualizes our discussion of the priest's acting *in persona Christi* at the eucharist. It was an insight that appeared quite novel to me in my doctoral student days, as I had been raised in a piety that said, "The priest celebrates Mass, the people receive communion." (Note that the first is an active verb, the second passive.)

A second starting point for viewing the issue of *in persona Christi* is to situate the role of the priest first within the larger context of the church. *Inter Insigniores,* the 1976 Vatican Declaration on Women in the Ministerial Priesthood, does not start this way. It states that it is Christ who must be represented sacramentally, and the priest is *the* sacramental sign of Christ, who is present as head and shepherd. It does not situate the priest immediately in the context of the church: "It is true that the priest represents the church, which is the Body of Christ. But if he does so, it is precisely because he first represents Christ himself, who is the head and shepherd of the church."[10]

On the level of sign, would it not be better to state that it is the liturgical action, not the priest, that is *the* sacramental sign? The role of the priest must be viewed first in relation to that action, and that liturgical action is one — that is, it is the action of the whole Christ, the *totus Christus,* head and members, in Saint Augustine's terms. The action of the body of the church *is* the action of Christ, and vice versa. David Power writes:

> More fundamental than the exclusion of women from order, then, is that of the relation between minister and community in all activities of the church, and most particularly in sacrament and worship. It is to be asked

whether it is not possible to see a unity, a oneness between Christ's action and that of the body, that overcomes the kind of differentiation that seems to hold the priest apart from the Body. One cue is found in Saint Thomas himself, in his image of Christ and church as one person.[11]

The official commentary on *Inter Insigniores* expressed a fear in relation to allowing a primary status to *in persona ecclesiae*, as it would make the priest simply a delegate of the community.[12] This fear, however, would not seem to follow necessarily if we were to keep in mind that when the priest acts *in persona ecclesiae*, he does so precisely as someone ordained not by the people but by Christ.

My third point of departure for a discussion of the issue of *in persona Christi* at the eucharist is a nuance of the same theme as the previously mentioned one: looking first to the *res* of the eucharist (the unity of the mystical body) rather than to the *res et sacramentum* (the real presence).

Many Catholics today see the chief role of the Mass as simply providing them with a validly consecrated host. Because of this, it is no wonder that communion services are being so readily accepted in Sunday celebrations in the absence of a priest. The matter needs to be contextualized in the broader vision of bringing about and effecting the communion in grace between Christ and the church, which is the heart of what eucharist is about.

The shift of emphasis from *res et sacramentum* to *res* calls for a shift in thinking as to just what role "sacrifice" plays in the meaning of the eucharist. In a recent work, David Power urges a demythologization of the language of priesthood and sacrifice. In his call for a language of reversal, we would view sacrifice less as a way to appease an angry God and more as something pointing to "a communion of solidarity in love in God's Spirit."[13]

This brings me to my fourth and final starting point. This is more of an experiential one, namely, how ordained ministers view themselves. In my 35 years of teaching I have seen a great deal of change in the view ordained ministers have of their ministerial actions in the church. I believe there is a great danger at the present moment of losing sight of the broader ecclesiological context of which we have been speaking. With a more narrow view of interpreting their acting *in persona Christi,* ordained ministers can be tempted to see themselves as the ones who confect the eucharist, with the presence of the people being something not that important or, in the extreme, even something accidental.

page 85

Some ministers avoid this extreme position and firmly believe that the eucharistic prayer is the prayer of the gathered assembly, but they put in brackets the words of the institution narrative. Here they step out of the prayer and "act as Jesus." Such an attitude underscores the important work that still needs to be done in studying the role of the institution narrative within the context of the eucharistic prayer.

Let me close by saying that in all our research on the role of the *in persona Christi* in the eucharist, we must contextualize our work within the entire Catholic tradition, embracing both West and East. Tradition tells us that a synergy is involved at the eucharist. Synergy was a classical term in patristic theology; it connoted a joint activity or combined energies between the human and the divine. Such a tradition effected an ecclesiology of communion that saw church as the communion of God with humanity. Every baptized member was to enter into the movement of this synergy. An over-reliance on the sole role of the ordained goes against this synergy that is the tradition of the eucharist: a joint activity, or combined energies between the Holy Spirit and *all* the baptized present under the leadership of the ordained minister.[14]

GERARD AUSTIN, OP

Endnotes

1. Bernard Dominique Marliangeas, "Clés pour une théologie du Ministère: *In Persona Christi, In Persona Ecclesiae,*" *Théologie Historique* 51 (Paris: Editions Beauchesne, 1978).

2. See *Worship* 63 (March 1989): 157–65; (September 1989): 467–73; *Worship* 65 (January 1991): 50–59; (May 1991): 263–68; *Worship* 66 (November 1992): 498–517; *Worship* 67 (May 1993): 269–78.

3. Dennis Michael Ferrara, "Representation or Self-Effacement? The Axiom *In Persona Christi* in St. Thomas and the Magisterium," *Theological Studies* 55 (1994): 195–224; Dennis Michael Ferrara, "The Ordination of Women: Tradition and Meaning," *Theological Studies* 55 (1994): 706–719; Sara Butler, "*Quaestio Disputata: In Persona Christi:* A Response to Dennis M. Ferrara," *Theological Studies* 56 (1995): 61–80; Dennis Michael Ferrara, "*In Persona Christi:* A Reply to Sara Butler," *Theological Studies* 56 (1995): 81–91.

4. David N. Power, "Representing Christ in Community and Sacrament," in *Being a Priest Today,* ed. Donald J. Goergen (Collegeville: Liturgical Press, 1992): 97–123.

5. David Coffey, "Priestly Representation and Women's Ordination," in *Priesthood: The Hard Questions,* ed. Gerald P. Gleeson (Newtown, NSW, Australia: E.J. Dwyer, 1993): 77–99.

6. Yves Congar, "L'Ecclesia ou communauté chrétienne, sujet intégral de l'action liturgique," in *La Liturgie après Vatican II,* Unam Sanctam 66, ed. J.P. Jossua and Y. Congar (Paris: Editions du Cerf, 1967): 241–82.

7. *Tractatus in evengelium Ioannis,* 21,8.

8. See Pierre-Marie Gy, "Le Nous de la prière eucharistique," *La Maison-Dieu* 191 (1992): 7–14.

9. Sermon 5 (PL 185: 57).

10. See *Origins* 6:33 (February 3, 1977): 523.

11. David N. Power, "Representing Christ," p. 114.

12. See *Origins,* 6:33, 524–31.

13. David Power, *The Eucharistic Mystery: Revitalizing the Tradition* (New York: Crossroad, 1992): 322.

14. See the important work of Jean Corbon, *The Wellspring of Worship* (New York: Paulist Press, 1988).

Liturgical Homily
Connecting the Body

MARY COLLINS, OSB

The homily is to be highly esteemed, as part of the liturgy itself" (SC, 52).[1] "The liturgical homily should have an exceptional place" in the ministry of the word (DV, 24). These official affirmations, one from the Second Vatican Council's Constitution on the Sacred Liturgy and the other from the Council's Constitution on Divine Revelation, remain in place. In the uneven reception of the liturgical reforms of Vatican II during the past 30 years, the restoration of the liturgical homily has not been seriously challenged.

Left unchallenged, the liturgical praxis of the homily also remains largely unexamined, seldom accorded critical reflection. The Catholic people do or do not like what they hear on any given Sunday from their liturgical presider. Homilists proceeding by trial and error and their hearers, pleased or disappointed, are largely unaware that good theory is key to improving the practice of the liturgical homily. Yet the lack of sound theory may underlie the chronic weakness in liturgical preaching that persists despite the church's conviction that the homily is a constitutive element of our eucharistic praxis.

Homiletics professor Robert Waznak has observed that as the postconciliar church, we may know less than we think we do about the kind of liturgical speaking the homily entails.[2] It is easy enough to understand the weakness in homiletic theory by checking the basic documentation: the liturgy constitution itself, the first general instruction for its implementation, other conciliar texts and the more recent *Catechism of the Catholic Church*. "Homily" appears with a minimum of explanation in conciliar texts, as though the retrieval of a long-dormant patristic genre was self-explanatory. The 1963 conciliar *Constitution on the Sacred Liturgy* mandates the restoration of the Sunday homily, stating that "by means of the homily the mysteries of the faith and the guiding principles of the Christian life are expounded from the sacred text during the course of the liturgical year" (sc, 52). Earlier in the same constitution, reference is made to "preaching" done in the liturgy, and there it is said that such preaching "should draw its content mainly from scriptural and liturgical sources, being a proclamation of God's wonderful works in the history of salvation, the mystery of Christ, ever present and active within us, especially in the celebration of the liturgy" (sc, 35). The assertions are vigorous, but their meaning is dense.

The First General Instruction *Inter Oecumenici*, issued in 1964 to guide the implementation of the recently promulgated liturgy constitution, offered some slight additional guidance in the form of a working definition and a caution.[3] One can hear behind the definition the straightforward pastoral question: What does the required homily entail? "A homily on the sacred texts means an explanation, pertinent to the mystery celebrated and the special needs of the listeners, of some point in either the reading from sacred scripture or in another text from the Ordinary or Proper of the day's Mass"

(10, 54). The caution, too, responds to a tacit query: What is the relationship of the genre *homilia* to the (then more familiar) syllabus for the annual sermon cycles on Catholic doctrine, Catholic moral life and the seven sacraments? "Because the homily is part of the liturgy for the day, any syllabus proposed for preaching within the Mass during certain periods must keep intact the intimate connection with at least the principal seasons and feasts of the liturgical year . . . , that is, with the mystery of redemption" (10, 55).

page 89

The 1965 conciliar decree *Presbyterium Ordinis,* on the life and ministry of priests, also speaks indirectly to the question of the homily when it takes up the matter of the priest as preacher. The text says that "the task of priests is not to teach their own wisdom, but God's Word, and to summon all [people] urgently to conversion and to holiness" (PO, 4). The text acknowledges immediately the cultural challenges priests face in effective preaching. "If it is to influence the mind of the listener more fruitfully . . . preaching must not present God's word in a general and abstract fashion only, but it must apply the perennial truth of the gospel to the concrete circumstances of life." That same concern for effective preaching of the gospel comes up again in *Eucharistiae participationem,* a 1973 circular letter from the Roman congregation to the presidents of episcopal conferences on the topic of eucharistic prayers.[4] The liturgical homily is mentioned in a discussion of how (without encroaching on the text of the eucharistic anaphora) the liturgy can be adapted to the needs of the celebrating community. The homily is identified as the part of the liturgy "by which the word of God proclaimed in the liturgical assembly is explained to help the community present. It is given in a way that is suited to the community's capacity and way of life and that is relevant to the circumstances of the celebration" (EP, 15).

Beyond offering that modest assistance about what is involved in the restoration of the homily, the first generation of liturgical reformers may have presumed that seminary professors would undertake the necessary formation of liturgical homilists, using as their models the great patristic figures who created the oral genre of the homily.[5]

MARY COLLINS, OSB

The 1994 *Catechism of the Catholic Church* (CCC), prepared as a reference book for a new generation of bishops thirty years after the Council, does not advance the discussion on the nature of the homily.[6] At times the CCC simply repeats themes already noted. At other times it seems to shift focus and thus narrow our understanding of the genre; it does this by tying the homily to the lectionary texts rather than to the saving mystery that the texts proclaim and the liturgy itself celebrates. Within an extended discussion of the movement of the church's eucharistic liturgy, the CCC describes the homily not as a hermeneutical exercise—an act of interpretation in a particular situation — but as a positivist "exhortation to accept this Word [the texts proclaimed in the liturgy of the word] as what it truly is, the Word of God, and to put it into practice" (CCC, 1349).

Even this brief comparison of descriptions of the liturgical homily formulated during the conciliar period with the more constricted presentation of the liturgical homily in the recent *Catechism of the Catholic Church* signals the need for a thorough exploration of the nature and purpose of the genre. This essay will make a contribution by trying to reframe Catholic understanding of the homily.

Robert Waznak, cited earlier, makes two points that will be developed here. First, Waznak emphasizes the complexity of "homily" as an oral genre; in its historical origins in the life of the church, the homily is public speech that is simultaneously biblical, liturgical, kerygmatic and familiar. Second, Waznak's review of history alerts us that the genre "homily" did not exist as a speech form among Catholic speakers of the English (or any other modern vernacular) language until 30 years ago. True, the church has ample documentation witnessing to the practice of the homily among speakers of Greek and Latin in the early Christian centuries,[7] but contemporary Catholic liturgical leaders — whether lay ministers with a pastoral charge, ordained presbyters, deacons and bishops, or those engaged in their ministerial formation — are in the process of creating the homily genre in our mother tongues, learning by doing. After commenting on each of these matters briefly, it will be possible to offer a fresh approach to the ongoing development of the genre "liturgical homily" in the United States.

The Homily as a Complex Genre

The first generation of English-language liturgical homilists and those of us *page 91* who have listened to their best efforts over the years are witnesses that the homily fails when the homilist makes the complex *simple;* yet reductionism is the recurring fault in current homiletic practice.

The homily is biblical. One common path to oversimplification is reducing the homily to explaining scripture. The Vatican II *Constitution on Divine Revelation (Dei Verbum),* 25, citing Augustine and Jerome, correctly stresses the importance of personal reading and disciplined study of scripture for all who exercise a ministry of the word in the church. A liturgical homilist ignorant of the biblical canon is *a priori* a failed homilist, since the story of the church is a continuation of the biblical story of salvation. Nevertheless, a homily reduced to its biblical component alone may be historical-critical exegesis, Bible study, biblical theology or *lectio divina* done in public; it is not yet a liturgical homily.

The homily is liturgical. Homilists proceed on a second reductionist path when they deceive themselves with flawed logic. A hidden syllogism maintains an argument something like this: Because a homily is a structural unit in the liturgical event, whatever the deacon, priest or bishop says at that structural moment functions as the day's homily. Such faulty reasoning has opened the way for many banal words, narcissistic tales, exercises in abstraction, appeals for funds and social commentaries to be spoken at this structural position. So also, many fine instructions on ecclesiastical topics have been delivered at this point in the Sunday liturgy, yet they have failed the liturgical assembly who sat waiting for the homily! A homily does not become such by virtue of the structural position of the spoken words. A genuine homily is liturgical speaking that uncovers the mystery present in people's lives and connects it with the mystery present sacramentally in the liturgical event.

MARY COLLINS, OSB

The homily is kergymatic. A successful homily cannot be reduced to the voicing of doctrinally correct sentences and sentiments about Jesus, the Spirit, the Father, the church. The "kerygmatic" word—a word announcing the good news of salvation—does something more than state the doctrines of the faith. What more? Long ago, I committed to memory one sentence from an otherwise forgotten New Testament scholar: "Not every word about God is the word of God, but only the word that sets us free to love." A word that moves hearts to love is a word of grace, a word of prophecy evoking conversion. How many homilists have spoken orthodox Christian words year in and year out, yet have failed to strike any chord but tedium—even in their own hearts! A homily reduced to doctrinal orthodoxy without kerygmatic power is a failed homily.

The homily is familiar. This is the quality that gives the liturgical unit its odd name, transposed from the Greek language spoken throughout the early Christian communities. *Homilia* is communion, intimate exchange, "familiar conversation." Remembering the origins of the technical name for this liturgical unit preserves something of immense significance for the contemporary church as it tries to retrieve and refashion the liturgical homily. The great Christian teachers of antiquity devised the Christian genre "homily" for speaking about the life of faith in the Christian liturgical assembly through concrete and particular acts of speaking in such settings. What needed inventing was an alternative to the available models of public speaking in Greek and Latin.

Many early bishops, educated men who had studied and even taught classical grammar and rhetoric, used these rhetorical models effectively in their civic and academic settings. They knew firsthand the fundamental inadequacy of classical forms of public speaking for the Christian liturgical assembly. They saw the need for alternatives. They developed their homiletic eloquence by interpreting the mystery of Christ in terms in which their own cultures could recognize its truth. The homily they invented for the liturgical assembly was "familiar" *relative to* the formality of civic and academic rhetoric. More significantly, the homily was also "familiar" *as the symbolic discourse* of people who had become intimates, one body filled with the one same Spirit, the church of Christ.

Why is advertence to the historical origins of the genre "homily" important? First, as we consider our contemporary rhetorical context, we know that late-twentieth-century American English is seldom spoken in ways that are identifiable as formal discourse, whether in academic or civic settings. We have little culturally normative "formality"—courts of law may be an exception—from which to depart in the interests of "familiar" speaking. Second, we recognize that public discourse in our secular society has no agreed-upon language for attending to the presence of mystery. Political debate, public commentary in the talk-show setting and media advertising as the language of commerce and entertainment all tend in the opposite direction, embarrassed by any transcendent reference.

page 93

Interpreting the liturgical homily as "familiar speech" without an accurate understanding of what "familiar" meant in its original context can lead to the erroneous judgment that the liturgical homily should emulate popular public discourse and be "familiar" in a common-sense understanding of the term. If not checked, such an error in understanding will eventually render the Catholic people incoherent. The church of Jesus Christ can hardly aspire to a ministry of the word in the liturgical assembly that is more casual, more blunt and less dignified than much ordinary speaking done in public places; yet some forays into popular culture to develop the homily as "familiar" speaking have produced the homilist whose liturgical speaking emulates the self-referential monologue of the talk-show host. Interpreting the homily as "familiar" speech on these faulty terms is another form of homiletic reductionism.

The liturgical homily is indeed a complex oral genre, yet once the church in the United States has the temerity to acknowledge what we have been struggling with for 30 years—our English language deficit in regard to the homily—we are at a new point of departure. The fault, egregious as it is, may not lie simply with individual homilists after all. A homilist who imitates the banter of the late-night host to speak of the gospel, the one who reverts to classroom biblical exegesis, the one who recites doctrinal texts from the *Catechism of the Catholic Church* or a papal encyclical—all are witnesses to our language deficit. No one form of reductionism is worse than the other; they all fall short of the goal.

Once we openly acknowledge this deficit, we can move beyond blaming the homilists and start rethinking the matter. The homily—complex in its balance of biblical, liturgical, kerygmatic and familiar aspects—needs to be inculturated. This appropriating of an ancient Christian oral genre for the contemporary liturgical event will not be accomplished by emulating the speech of popular culture, nor by repeating the rhetoric of the magisterium or of the classroom lecture. It will come from a contemporary transformation of the historical datum that the homily is essentially the "familiar" speaking Christians do in the liturgical assembly.

Rethinking the Homily

The liturgical homily is a part of the church's tradition worth retrieving; but the tradition is living, so restoration is not mere imitation. The church of the apostles and the church of classical antiquity went beyond available forms of oral discourse, transforming available language to preach Christ Jesus and the dawning reign of God. On the edge of the third Christian millennium, we must emulate their project, not their product.

We can enter the inculturation process only by speaking and listening to one another as the Body of Christ in this cultural reality, for the homily is a proclamation of the mystery that we are. Because the liturgical homily is speaking done as we celebrate "our own mystery" (in Saint Augustine's oft-cited phrase), we must first be able to name how the mystery is at work among us as the Catholic church in the United States. Our reality is not simply that we are English-speaking, Spanish-speaking, polyglot and "multicultural." As Catholics living in the United States on the crest of the third Christian millennium, we are also part of a pseudo-secular society unready or unable to name publicly what theologian Karl Rahner described as "the Whither of transcendence."[8]

page 95

Our American democratic individualism holds in tension egalitarian impulses and plutocratic institutions. We are blessed and victimized by our technological inventiveness. We are generous philanthropists and avaricious consumers of the world's goods. We are part of a society that indulges and abuses its children, and is stunned at their violence and alienation. We cannot be Catholic Christians in some abstract universal way; we are the Catholic church in relation to this cultural world that shapes our bodies, our desires, our fears, our aspirations, our imaginations. Still, the mystery of Christ which the liturgy celebrates is somehow already present in this cultural world, or there is no reason to celebrate at all.

The homily-inventing world of "the church fathers" enjoyed different cultural achievements and was weighed down with different burdens. Melito of Sardis, Cyril of Jerusalem, John Chrysostom and Augustine—eloquent as they were in preaching Christ in the dying Roman empire—would be speechless in North America today; yet this is the milieu in which the Spirit is speaking to this particular church. We have no choice but to reinvent the homiletic genre for this complex cultural situation within which the flame of faith burns and flickers among the Catholic people. The stakes in the retrieval of the liturgical homily are high. How can the Spirit poured out in Christian baptism as the power for salvation find public voice among us in our Sunday assemblies?

Inculturation theory alerts us to recognize that inculturation of the homily, like any authentic inculturation, is not simply a task for the ordained to grapple with.[9] It is a process in which the whole church must participate if the liturgical homily is to be effectively retrieved for this cultural situation. Wise pastors are already "listening the laity into authentic speech" about their faith and hope—and about their incredulity. Wise pastors are listening to the voices of the alienated and marginalized as well as the engaged churchgoers.

They are gathering up the fragments of grace and ambiguity, hope and anxiety, conviction and confusion named within ordinary speech and discordant public discourse. What these wise pastors are gathering are seedlings for whatever the liturgical homily must become. The mature genre will be harvested from the text and texture of ordinary Christian lives. God is not afraid of us and does not despise us; the Holy Spirit breathes here.

This confidence is "a Catholic thing"; yet despite confidence in "God with us," the post-conciliar church in the United States is only beginning to fashion the homily as an effective vehicle for liturgical proclamation of the mystery of Christ present. Neither the best pastoral renewal program for the ordained nor the best homiletics class in the best seminary can package what we do not yet have. There is work to be done. The norm for judging our liturgical praxis is the evangelical vitality of the church.

A generation ago, an impulse to develop the homiletic genre produced the phenomenon of the "dialogue homily." This form was typically undisciplined and unfocused; its general demise implies a consensus that it failed as a life-giving word. The impulse itself was an expression of people's desire, however awkward, to give voice to their concerns in the presence of the mystery manifest in the liturgy. Honoring that admittedly undisciplined and unsuccessful impulse to connect liturgy and life suggests a way forward.

Continuing aspiration for an inculturated homily will require more intentional collaboration between the pastors and the members of the Body of Christ. What form will this collaboration take? Some local communities are already devising ways to listen one another into authentic speaking about the power of the gospel for salvation in this culture. Base communities and Womenchurch come to mind. An ecclesial version of the "focus group" is another model, as when those charged with pastoral office sustain their homily preparation by reflecting regularly on liturgical texts with some of their gathered parishioners, whether these parishioners are identifiable as parish leaders, the marginalized or the dutiful. The talk—in season and out—must address what is going on in the liturgy and what is going on in people's ordinary lives, and how these interpret one another. The conversation frames of reference will include households, communities, the larger social units of nation and world community and the church itself, which mediates Catholic Christian identity.

Occasionally, pastors may succeed in pressing the laity beyond conventional Catholic religious discourse, freeing them to speak of the tensions between the confident majesty of the liturgy and the raw edges of their lives of faith. Occasionally, people will so press their pastors that tongues tied by ecclesial and social convention are freed to speak an authentically evangelical invitation to freedom in Christ.[10] In these intentional settings, the best outcome would be that everyone listens well and that at least some take what they hear to prayer and then return to the group less guarded and more attentive to what is occurring among them. I suggest that what is being manifested in such a process is the church trying to give voice to the Spirit speaking within. The inculturated liturgical homily is being conceived in such an ecclesial matrix.

Toward theoretical foundation. The integrity of the process for inculturating the liturgical homily described here can be substantiated through the work of many theoreticians, two of whom can be alluded to here. French theologian Louis Marie Chauvet, in his work *Symbol and Sacrament,* provides one source for understanding why the whole church and not just the clergy must take part in revitalizing the liturgical homily. The homily, as a liturgical act, is symbolic speaking done in the Christian community. As such it works effectively not at the level of cognition, where information is exchanged and ideas are explored, but at the level of recognition, where the speaking touches us "to the quick,"[11] revealing us to ourselves. Because we are vulnerable at the quick, symbolic speech has the power to move us.

By contrast, speech that is deliberately inauthentic, but also everyday patterns of language, work to mask, protect and manipulate that living core, offering us instead a familiar and orderly world to live in. Even conventionalized uses of once-powerful religious language can deliberately shield us from the presence of the saving mystery. These two — the public rhetoric of our secular, technological, consumer society and conventionalized God-talk— both aim to get us to settle for less than fullness of life in Christ Jesus, which is unavoidably paschal, requiring transformation through conversion.

The homily, as symbolic language used in the liturgical celebration of the mystery of salvation, must aim "to the quick," not dodge it. Further, the homily is symbolic speech addressed not only to the individuals who are the members of the ecclesial body but also to the whole assembly gathered as the Body of Christ. In order to address the church in the fullness of its mystery, the homilist and community together must locate the ecclesial "quick" in all its multiple sites. The church must risk opening itself to the "two-edged sword" that is the word of God as the precondition for the gift of good homilies. En route to inculturating the homily, ecclesial communities must recognize and name for themselves their numbness and their pain, their reasons for gratitude and joy. Only then can ordinary life be brought to the light of Christ. We know already that men in pastoral office cannot do this naming alone. Miriam's question echoes across the generations: "Is it through Moses alone that Yahweh speaks? Does God not speak through us also?" (Numbers 12:2). The homilist who is familiar with the concrete faith of the faith community is the one prepared to speak a word that is at once biblical, liturgical, kergymatic and intimate.

Julia Kristeva's psychoanalytic studies of language provide additional theory in support of this proposed path toward the inculturation of the homily.[12] She points out that hidden in the deep structure of our ordinary speaking, but not evident in the overt surfaces of the language we have learned to speak, lie the unconscious traces of our primal drives and aspirations. These are socially and culturally subdued in the interests of good public order, even good ecclesial order. In this process, some of "the good that we would do"[13] is as likely to be submerged as are the darker, self-destructive and socially destructive impulses that we have learned to fear. Powerful symbols—the symbols of art, dreams, music, biblical narrative and cultural stories—help us connect our conscious and our unconscious selves.

Effective symbols move us to the edge of mystery, where the urge for communion and the impulse toward death draw us. Beyond social and religious convention, beyond social and religious alienation, lies the invitation to paschal life in Christ if we can learn to recognize this as "good news." Effective symbolic communication in the liturgical assembly can make it possible for Catholic communities to risk moving beyond what seems safe because it is familiar. Effective symbolic communication can invite communities to move more surely into the mystery of death and life in Christ in this place and time.

page 99

Kristeva's important reflections on language suggest further that the effective homilist will be one who has listened to the silences as well as to the words of the ordinary speaking that other people do, and then has listened to the resonant echo of the silence within. Only then can the biblical word come into that silence by the power of the Holy Spirit in order to take shape again as a liturgical proclamation of the mystery of Christ. When the homily emerges in this way, it will reveal sin and grace in terms quite familiar to the community. Recognition will come, and with it, the possibility of transformation.

Chauvet and Kristeva taken together point up the real demands placed on a liturgical homilist who would proclaim the mystery of Christ and the Spirit of Christ at work in the world. Any homilist who hopes to speak with power is dependent both on what is said to expose "the quick" of particular ecclesial communities and also on what is concealed in that church's silences, even in the liturgical forms themselves. Given this theory as a point of departure, "familiar" as a characteristic of the homily is not primarily a matter of establishing an appropriate rhetorical or personal style. "Familiar" is not about "style" at all. It is substance, not eloquence, and the church recognizes the difference. With or without human eloquence, when homilists speak in the assembly in such a way that the Catholic people of the United

States can recognize themselves, sinful and Spirit-filled in the speaking, the eucharistic Body of Christ will connect. Then the inculturated homily will have begun to emerge in this church.

Endnotes

1. Translations of conciliar documents are from *The Documents of Vatican II,* ed. Walter Abbott (New York: America Press, 1966).

2. Robert Waznak, "Homily," in *The New Dictionary of Sacramental Worship,* ed. Peter Fink (Collegeville, MN: The Liturgical Press, 1990): 552–58.

page 101

3. *Inter Oecumenici* (September 26, 1964), *Acta Apostolicae Sedis* (1964): 877–900. English translation in *Documents on the Liturgy 1963–79* (hereafter DOL), trans. International Commission on English in the Liturgy (Collegeville, MN: Liturgical Press, 1982): 88–110.

4. *Eucharistiae participationem* (April 27, 1973), in *Notitiae* 9 (1973): 193–201. English translation: DOL, pp. 623–29.

5. *Constitution on the Sacred Liturgy,* 14–18.

6. *Catechism of the Catholic Church* (Rome: Libreria Editrice Vaticana), trans. United States Catholic Conference (Mahway, N.J.: Paulist Press, 1994). The English language index is uneven in its reference to "homily." See paragraphs 1100, 1154, 1349, 1482, 1688, where explicit reference is made to the genre "homily." See also 1074, 1099, 1101, 1122, 1133, 1177, 1190, 1348, 1480, 1518.

7. The written texts of patristic homilies cannot be taken as fully reliable witnesses to actual oral delivery. The difference in oral and written presentations can be confirmed by anyone who has first addressed a group and then been asked to submit the talk as a text for publication.

8. Karl Rahner, "The Concept of Mystery in Catholic Theology," *Theological Investigations* IV (New York: Seabury Press, 1974): 49ff.

9. Anscar J. Chupungco explores inculturation theory in *Liturgical Inculturation* (Collegeville, MN: The Liturgical Press, 1992).

10. On the freedom of the Christian, see Paul's letters to the Galatians and Romans, and Paul's many commentators.

11. Louis-Marie Chauvet, *Symbol and Sacrament: A Sacramental Reinterpretation of Christian Existence (Symbole et Sacrement: Un relecture sacramentelle de l'existence chrétienne* [Paris: Cerf, 1987]), trans. Patrick Madigan and Madeleine Beaumont (Collegeville, MN: The Liturgical Press): 123.

12. Julia Kristeva, *Revolution in Poetic Language* (New York: Columbia University Press, 1984); for an introductory discussion on Kristeva and theology, see Cleo McNelly Kearns, "Kristeva and Feminist Theology," in C. W. Maggie Kim et al., *Transfigurations: Theology and the French Feminists* (Minneapolis: Fortress Press, 1993): 55ff.

13. Paul gives an existential account of the tension in Romans 7:15–25.

Pastoral Ecumenism
The Common Lectionary

FREDERICK R. McMANUS

On a recent Sunday, eucharistic liturgies were celebrated by members of neighboring Catholic, Lutheran, Presbyterian, Disciples of Christ and other churches, listening to and celebrating the word of God with the same passages or excerpts from the scriptures. In both Catholic and other communities, this was an ecumenical fruit of the Second Vatican Council, one not directly planned, one not yet widely enough appreciated.[1]

At Sunday Mass in Catholic communities, the three readings that day were Exodus 32:7–11,13–14; 1 Timothy 1:12–17; and Luke 15:1–32 or 1–10 (the longer or shorter texts, respectively). In the other churches, there were slight differences: the first reading from Exodus restored the omitted verse 12 for completeness; the shorter gospel reading from Luke was appointed because it is complete in itself. In addition, the alternative of Jeremiah 4:11–12, 22–28 was another possible (and perhaps preferable) Old Testament reading.

Behind this list of chapter and verse numbers lies an extraordinary ecumenical convergence, a kind of pastoral, local or "quiet" ecumenism. It is the increasing use of the Roman liturgy's table of Sunday readings by the other churches in the adapted form called *The Revised Common Lectionary*.[2] The development goes far beyond the token or the symbolic.

No one should denigrate the significance of a meeting between the pope of Rome and the ecumenical patriarch of Constantinople or of the pope of Rome and the archbishop of Canterbury. These are great and grand events. Similarly, the scholarly dialogue and agreed statements of bilateral theological commissions are of high ecumenical importance. Yet on the local and real level, it is wrong to minimize the sense that Catholics or Lutherans, Presbyterians or Methodists may have that their Christian neighbors in the next parish are proclaiming and hearing the same plan of readings from God's word.

To this parallel liturgical celebration of the word have been added some providential side effects: common study groups of believers, joint homily preparation by preachers, publication of commentaries shared among the churches, some influence upon church calendars, even the use of the lectionary as a sound basis for curricula of Christian religious education.[3] It is concrete, real, living ecumenism.

The direct background is this: In 1969, the Catholic church published an innovative arrangement of biblical readings for Sunday Mass in the Roman rite of the Latin church. If there are close to a billion believers within the full Roman communion, the impact of this lectionary was massive and extraordinary. Of the huge numbers of Catholic Christians, fewer than twenty million do not follow the Roman liturgy, chiefly those who belong to the Eastern Catholic churches.

Whatever the numbers of Catholic Christians who actually and regularly gather for the eucharist on the Lord's day—25 percent, 50 percent, perhaps more—it would be hard to exaggerate the breadth and potential effect of this new plan of readings. It was in force worldwide at the end of November 1969. By itself, this meant that on Sundays, Catholics would hear and celebrate the word of God in richer, more generous, more diverse passages than had been possible since the early centuries when the inspired word was first read to Christians in their eucharistic assemblies. Whatever the reported dissatisfaction with homiletic preaching in the past quarter century, at the very least, preaching has been, surely and vastly, better-oriented to the scriptures themselves.

page 105

Rather overlooked in 1969, at least publicly, was the ecumenical potential of this Roman reform. Every Christian body, including the Catholic church, understandably looks at ecumenical undertakings, bilateral, multilateral or universal, from the perspective of its own contribution. It is a shared hope that each communion may add its distinctive dimensions—and positive ones at that—all the while gaining reciprocally from the religious perspectives of the other Christian churches and the working of the Holy Spirit in them.

One major Catholic contribution resulted in the ecumenical Sunday *Common Lectionary* of 1983, now *The Revised Common Lectionary* of 1992. Paradoxically, this adapted table of readings for Sunday celebrations is not used in the Catholic community at large; but more of that later.

The origin of the enterprise was of course in the Second Vatican Council and in its carrying out by Pope Paul VI. In 1963 the conciliar decree on the liturgy made a basic assertion: "It is essential to promote [in the liturgy] that warm and living love for the Scripture to which the venerable tradition of both eastern and western rites gives testimony."[4] In all candor, that love had not been much promoted in the preconciliar Roman liturgy. The goal became concrete in two significant ways.

FREDERICK R. MCMANUS

The first way was general: more reading from scripture in all services of worship, with selections that are more varied and appropriate. This is the origin of the innovation, or revolution, in the Catholic liturgical reform that added the reading of scripture to services as significant as baptism, marriage, penance and anointing, and to services as minor as the blessing of objects of religious devotion.

The second decision was still more important, because it affected the weekly liturgical assembly, to which the council directed its special attention: The pattern of the Sunday eucharist was to be radically altered. "The treasures of the Bible are to be opened up more lavishly [especially at Sunday Mass], so that a richer share in God's word may be provided for the faithful. In this way a more representative portion of holy scripture will be read to the people in a prescribed period of years"[5] (SC, 51).

This was the genesis of the 1969 Roman order of readings for Mass. A comparable pattern was also to be followed for weekday eucharistic celebrations and for the daily prayer office or Liturgy of the Hours. These other lists of readings, valuable in themselves, affect only the smallest fraction of Catholics and are of limited interest to most other Christian churches.

Today a diminishing minority can recall when the only regular contact most Catholic believers had with the Bible was the supplementary English reading of the gospel (and sometimes the epistle pericope) after the Latin at Sunday Mass. Preconciliar congregations never heard the Old Testament on Sundays. In many cases, even the gospel reading in English sounded like an afterthought; often it did not even begin to influence the preaching that followed.

The commission that was entrusted by Paul VI with the specifics of liturgical reform undertook the broadest study of lectionary arrangements, from early Christian usage to contemporary proposals, Western and Eastern, Catholic and not.[6] Some fifty tables or lists were studied before the basic decisions were taken. The whole process is recounted by the genius of the reform, Annibale Bugnini, in his history of the revision.[7]

The point of the undertaking was evident. On the one hand, there is nothing inspired, sacrosanct or absolute about any particular choice of biblical readings for Sunday celebrations. On the other hand, some patterns are better than others, and even then, these can always be refined and improved in the light of experience and in accommodation to the culture and cir-

page 107

cumstances. The Sunday lectionary, like the church itself, stands in need of continual reform.[8]

All the features of the Roman arrangement of 1969 — only slightly altered in a 1981 edition — deserve detailed examination, but the chief achievement was to increase more than three or four times the quantity, not to say quality, of the scriptures heard and celebrated by the people who follow the Roman Sunday liturgy. All scripture is inspired of God, but in the choice of excerpts, there is an evident hierarchy of religious values, significance of meaning or impact, and appropriateness to assembly or occasion.

As is well known, the reformed Roman rite's lectionary is based on a three-year cycle of gospel texts. In the ancient tradition of three readings at the Sunday eucharist—prophet, apostle, gospel—the third reading was judged the most significant but not necessarily the governing or controlling. The new cycle follows the three synoptic gospels in a so-called semicontinuous sequence, with some of the gospel according to John in the year otherwise devoted to the shortest synoptic, the gospel according to Mark. Old Testament readings have been introduced into Sunday use, ordinarily with some relation to the day's appointed gospel text. The New Testament readings are given in second place, including the letters of Paul and other writers of the apostolic period, and in their own semicontinuous pattern or sequence, independent of the gospel except in the great seasons of Advent-Christmas and Lent-Easter.

Much more could be said about the efforts to recover and improve venerable traditions, although not for mere archeological reasons: one, the threefold scheme of prophet, apostle and gospel, the other, semicontinuous readings. The goal, very much in the minds of the redactors, was the fuller and better proclamation of the word in the eucharistic assembly on the Lord's Day as a worshipful celebration of the deeds of God, a celebration also appropriate as a model for the most traditional catechesis of the Christian people. For the great seasons of Advent-Christmas and Lent-Easter, the festal or thematic tradition of the universal church was respected but with additional, more expansive choices of readings. The primary Christian festal observance, however, is the Lord's Day, which has historical, liturgical and pastoral priority over even the major seasons and feasts.[9] Special thought was given to the Sundays of so-called Ordinary Time, the periods after the Christmas and Easter seasons, respectively. This season or time *per annum* comprises two-thirds of the Sundays of the year—each one of which celebrates the paschal mystery of the Lord's death and resurrection.

The heart of the Roman pattern is, as already mentioned, the cycle of three years following Matthew, Mark and Luke. Here, and in other parts of the lectionary, much attention is paid to the semicontinuous reading from an individual book of the Bible. This is done only partly out of respect for what is understood to have been the practice of the first three or four centuries of Christian usage, namely, to take up a given gospel or letter or Old Testament book and simply read through it, week after week, celebration after celebration.

When selective lists of pericopes were drawn up to show what passages were designated to be read, it was clear enough that the Bible could not be read in its totality at the Sunday eucharist. Following the canonical text of each book of the scriptures, without attempting to put a scholastic, didactic or analytical cast on the choice of excerpts, has seemed the wiser choice, leaving the plan or sequence of the individual biblical books intact.

Behind this there is a principle: The word of God is proclaimed in the assembly not as a directly didactic or catechetical enterprise but as celebration. In a way, it is an act of faith to read the unadorned scriptures, choosing or selecting only as necessary but leaving to the divine word its own impact upon the human spirit of those who gather as the church of God.

PASTORAL ECUMENISM: THE COMMON LECTIONARY

In the choice of readings, done under Paul vi and published in 1969, there was some fruitful non-Roman ecumenical influence. The lectionary tables of the other churches were carefully studied, both historical precedents and contemporary proposals. Through the presence of a half dozen representatives of other churches in the work of the commission of implementation, one worry was eliminated: The other communions would welcome the Roman effort; in some cases they were already pursuing the same broad goals.

page 109

The happy result was the 1969 *Order of Readings of Mass,* a full list of texts (second edition in 1981, with some added biblical passages) that formed one section of the Roman Missal project.[10] It is this list that the volumes of current Catholic "lectionaries" follow today, with the complete readings printed in one or another translation.

Something else followed, unexpected but truly providential. In North America and gradually in other parts of the English-speaking Christian world, the Roman lectionary list was welcomed, adapted and adopted or permitted by mainline churches—even in some communities that lacked any real history of an appointed, fixed list of readings distributed through the church year.

In the United States, the ecumenical process began within a year of the Roman publication. *Worshipbook – Services* of the Presbyterian churches appeared in 1970, quickly followed by the Episcopal and Lutheran churches, Disciples of Christ and United Church of Christ, and finally a common list prepared by the Consultation on Church Union in 1974.[11] All this amounted to a kind of ecumenical reception of the Roman reform with adaptations to the specifics of different church calendars and traditions. The other communities thus welcomed the new order not merely as something to be admired but as a model to be adopted or allowed with lesser variations.

We cannot exaggerate how significant this development was. The papal commission preparing the Roman order of Sunday readings had worried lest its preempting the field might offend other churches, and every effort was made to avoid this. Two examples: The fears of German Catholic liturgical scholars that the Lutheran church in Germany would regard the new lectionary as an affront to their tradition of several centuries were resolved. A representative sent by the archbishop of Canterbury on behalf of the worldwide Anglican communion explained the positive interest of those churches in the Roman undertaking, since they were themselves similarly engaged.[12]

The next step, after the several adaptations in the mainline churches just mentioned, was a common enterprise, agreed upon in 1978 by the (North American) Consultation on Common Texts, known as CCT. This body, with participants from more than a dozen churches or church agencies, had already set in motion the process that led to the international *Prayers We Have in Common* (1975), from which came the shared use of texts for the creeds, the Gloria and Sanctus of the eucharist, and so on. In this, and in the lectionary study, there was full Catholic participation, especially that of the International Commission on English in the Liturgy (ICEL), in accord with its 1964 mandate from all the sponsoring conferences of Catholic bishops.

A study done for the North American CCT proposed that the proliferation of adapted lists of readings, all derived from the Roman order but with distinct characteristics, should be redacted into a single list with the help of biblical and liturgical scholars of diverse traditions. The result was the 1983 *Common Lectionary,* widely accepted for trial use during the next six years, that is, during two lectionary cycles. Then, after exhaustive study, a reworked pattern—still faithful to the Roman order of Sunday readings as its basis and source—appeared in 1992 as *The Revised Common Lectionary,* again with full Catholic participation.[13]

Admittedly, the common pattern is an adaptation with many variants but without substantial departure from the basic Roman order of readings. Some variations in the final product are refinements, such as filling out readings that seem to have become disjointed or are too selective of verses within a given biblical excerpt. In other cases, pericopes have been augmented by introductory or concluding biblical verses. A particular problem of great contemporary concern has been the inclusion of certain neglected readings dealing with the women of the scriptures. Following a policy introduced into contemporary Western liturgies under Pope John XXIII, greater sensitivity is shown in the case of passages that grate on twentieth-century ears as apparently anti-Semitic.

page 111

All in all, the variations or adaptations from the Roman list are not substantial, but one exception is worth mentioning. For the Old Testament readings in the periods after Pentecost or after Trinity Sunday, now called the Sundays in Ordinary Time in Roman terminology, a different selection is provided by the ecumenical lectionary. Even here, however, in the 1992 revision the extensive set of substitutions (like 2 Jeremiah for Exodus in the example already mentioned) is given simply as an alternative program.

The reasons are a little complex. The Roman plan respected the so-called semicontinuous sequence from Sunday to Sunday in the season of Ordinary Time, but not fully. Instead, Old Testament readings for that period of the year were chosen because of some relationship of theme or reference corresponding to the day's gospel—often a help to preachers as they try to choose one from among the several topics of any individual Sunday. This relationship frequently seems artificial or incidental, even a contrived or far-fetched typology, as both Catholic and Protestant scholars have objected. Moreover, it has the effect of leaving significant areas of the Old Testament untouched. (This is compensated for in the Roman readings at weekday Masses or in the daily Liturgy of the Hours, but of course relatively few people hear such readings.)

In a 1993 document, this very problem was acknowledged by the Pontifical Biblical Commission.[14] While generally praising the reformed Roman lectionary, the papal commission expressed some doubt: "By regularly associating a text of the Old Testament with the text of the gospel, the [Roman lectionary] cycle often suggests a scriptural interpretation moving in the direction of typology. But, of course, such is not the only kind of interpretation possible."[15]

FREDERICK R. MCMANUS

Anticipating this Roman cautionary note by several years, the 1983 *Common Lectionary* and its 1992 revision propose an alternative series for the first of the Sunday readings in Ordinary Time. This alternative series does follow a semicontinuous pattern, and it provides larger selections of historical or narrative texts from individual Old Testament books over a period of weeks but without much direct or formal relationship to the respective gospel texts. In a sense, this option is in even closer accord with the basic Roman principle of reading a given book of the Bible in a semicontinuous fashion. Here again, however, the Roman origin of the ecumenical effort is respected in *The Revised Common Lectionary,* and the individual Old Testament passages related to the gospel passages are still included as an alternative set.

The importance of a list of passages, as distinct from a full lectionary with readings spelled out, also deserves comment. Although the Roman lectionary also appeared first as a simple list (from which came full books of texts called lectionaries), Catholics are not usually familiar with the use of a "pulpit Bible," a pragmatic and traditional practice in some other churches. This is simply the full Bible, from which the reader or minister proclaims the texts that may be marked as appointed for a given celebration.

Although somewhat less convenient for the readers themselves, a list or order of readings rather than a book of readings has several advantages, an obvious one being that it is less costly to revise and republish periodically. It is, besides, more easily accommodated to the freer choice of biblical translations in actual liturgical celebration. For example, 20 years ago the American episcopate wisely approved three versions of the scriptures for Catholic liturgical use: the New American Bible, the Jerusalem Bible and the Catholic edition of the Revised Standard Version. This diversity—and it could be broader—has pastoral importance: A translation is only a translation, and the Christian people should not be misled by a seemingly sacrosanct single version. So far as translations are concerned, the *Common Lectionary* may be followed equally with the King James version, the Ronald Knox translation and that most admirable New Revised Standard Version.

There is still another dimension. Since lectionary lists, including the Roman, can be used with any appropriate version of the scriptures, there is no special reason why the project of a common, ecumenical list or order has to be confined to English-speaking churches, where the ecumenical plan originated. Credit goes to the initiatives of the English language group, but now fresh efforts have been made to move to wider use in other languages through overtures of the English Language Liturgical Consultation (ELLC).

page 113

This body is international and ecumenical, made up of representatives of official liturgical-ecumenical committees in countries around the world, including Catholic commissions. As the successor to the International Consultation on Common Texts (ICET), it first revised the common liturgical texts of that body and published them in 1992.[16] Now ELLC has taken steps to promote *The Revised Common Lectionary* for use in languages other than English. The first major effort occurred at the August 1993 congress of Societas Liturgica in Fribourg, Switzerland. There, scholars of different churches and languages, especially German and French, had a solid introduction to the common list as a table of readings that is equally available to any language group.

Immediately afterward, ELLC had its own meeting in Geneva at the headquarters of the World Council of Churches. The occasion was used to meet informally with representatives of several bodies, from the Faith and Order Commission of the WCC to the Lutheran World Federation to the World Alliance of Reformed Churches. Again the point was made and accepted that the lectionary pattern developed ecumenically from the Roman order should be studied in any and all language groups of Christian communities.

In May 1994, the steering committee of ELLC, headed by Professor Horace Allen of the Boston University School of Theology and Father John Fitzsimmons, a parish priest and biblical scholar from Scotland, met in Rome. Again ELLC took the occasion to seek broader interest outside the English language world, this time at informal meetings with the Pontifical

Council for Promoting Christian Unity and the Congregation for Divine Worship and the Discipline of the Sacraments.

These meetings were prompted in part by the explicit recommendation in the pontifical council's revision of the Roman ecumenical directory, page 114 approved by Pope John Paul II in early 1993.[17] This document encourages efforts to employ common agreed liturgical texts, such as the Lord's Prayer, the creeds, Gloria, Sanctus, etc.—ecumenical enterprises long since achieved in large parts of the English-speaking world, including the Catholic church. It also recommends joint efforts in hymnbooks, music and the translation of the psalms, and it has a direct reference to lectionaries, saying that "a similar agreement for common scriptural readings for liturgical use should also be explored," precisely the point and purpose of the *Common Lectionary* itself.[18]

Almost as important a Roman development, again in the preceding year, was a direct reference to the matter in the Pontifical Biblical Commission's 1993 statement on biblical interpretation in the church, already mentioned. The text praises the reformed Roman lectionary of 1969 (with some reservation) and then expresses satisfaction at its ecumenical impact: "Even as it [the Roman lectionary] stands, it has had positive ecumenical effects."[19] Once again, it is the achievement of the *Common Lectionary* that is recorded and welcomed.

With this background the 1994 ELLC meetings with the Roman departments were highly successful, but behind them lies a curious history. Not long after the first edition of the *Common Lectionary* was published in 1983, the National Conference of Catholic Bishops voted in favor of its trial use in a hundred or so parishes in the United States. On the face of it, this seemed to be a limited and cautious experiment fully in accord with the terms of the Roman lectionary. It was a good deal less an adaptation than the radical omission of one of the first two readings at Sunday Mass, a matter already within the competence of the conferences of bishops.[20] Such an experiment with the *Common Lectionary* was both liturgical and ecumenical, or so it seemed. It was an improved lectionary directly based on the Roman table of readings and shared with other churches.

At that time the application was denied by the competent Roman department for rather weak reasons. One was the alleged threat to the "uniformity" of the Roman rite, although Vatican II had been completely satisfied with the broad "unity" of the rite;[21] in fact, the ecumenical lectionary plan positively supported unity within Catholic usage. A second problem was the asserted elimination of passages from the deutero-canonical or apocryphal books, although fewer than ten such texts had been first introduced into Roman usage only in 1969; they were still available for Catholic use in the *Common Lectionary*. Finally, opposition from the Secretariat for Promoting Christian Unity was reported; in fact, the Secretariat supported the enterprise.

page 115

This complicated Roman position made it impossible for Catholics in the American church and elsewhere to share in an authorized experiment with the 1983 *Common Lectionary* itself. The situation was ironic and paradoxical, since it was the Roman lectionary that was being widely shared among the other churches in the common venture.

A new climate may now be hoped for, in light of the meetings just mentioned and in view of the 1993 Roman encouragement to common lectionaries, both in the ecumenical directory and in the document on interpretation of the Bible. This may lead ultimately, in some places, to a formal use of *The Revised Common Lectionary* as such in the Catholic community, with the requisite authorizations. At the least, the ecumenical adaptation of the Roman lectionary can prove invaluable as the Roman order itself is developed and further revised. Ideally there could be official, ongoing, worldwide, multinational, multilanguage and ecumenical dialogue on a lectionary for common use on Sundays.

The promotional work of ELLC continued in 1996, too: first at the congress of Societas Liturgica in Dublin in August, and then at its own meeting in Carlow at the Irish Institute of Pastoral Liturgy, with the participation of observers from outside the English-language countries. A positive side-effect of the whole undertaking appeared in the ELLC discussions at Carlow: wider ecumenical interest in prayer texts composed with some reference to the readings of the three-year Sunday lectionary. The representatives of other churches used the occasion to praise the insights, quality and potential of the new ICEL alternative opening prayers for Sunday Mass. Inspired by the biblical readings of the respective days, these original texts were prepared by ICEL under its mandate and have been submitted to the participating conferences of Catholic bishops.

To return to the lectionary proper, a further possibility that the departments of the Roman curia will be moved to a favorable reappraisal of *The Revised Common Lectionary* is found in an oblique, but very positive, reference in the recent encyclical letter of Pope John Paul, *Ut unum sint* (May 25, 1995): "Corresponding to the liturgical renewal carried out by the Catholic church, certain other ecclesial communities have made efforts to renew their worship. . . . Again, when the cycles of liturgical readings used by the various Christian communities in the West are compared, they appear to be essentially the same."[22] The deep Catholic involvement in the preparation of *The Revised Common Lectionary* and what seems to be a recurring attention paid to it by the Roman See, at least in principle and as ideal, may move particular churches in the Catholic communion in the same direction.

Even without such providential developments, today's situation is already a remarkable sign of ecumenical convergence. That we can hear God's word in a pattern substantially common is a clear blessing for pastoral ecumenical activity. It may simply be in the common recognition that we share week by week in the hearing of God's word according to a common or very similar pattern. It may be in the ways in which preachers and people explore the scriptures together. It may be in the quiet ecumenism of one less barrier between the churches—and this in the blessed area of the inspired scriptures celebrated in the Sunday eucharist.

Endnotes

1. An 800-word précis of this paper appeared in *Commonweal* on January 13, 1995.

2. *The Revised Common Lectionary: Includes Complete List of [Sunday] Lections for Years A, B, and C,* ed. Consultation on Common Texts (Nashville, TN: Abingdon Press; Winfield, B.C.: Wood Lake Books; Norwich, England: Canterbury Press, 1992). For an excellent bibliography on lectionary developments since Vatican II, see Fritz West, "An Annotated Bibliography on the Three-year Lectionaries: Part I: The Roman Catholic Lectionary," *Studia Liturgica* 23 (1993): 223–44; "Parts II–IV," 24 (1994): 222–48.
page 117

3. Unfortunately the writers of the *Catechism of the Catholic Church* (English editions, 1994) rejected alternative and venerable patterns of catechesis and apparently never considered the schema of the Roman lectionary for the Sunday celebration of the word of God as the basis for catechesis. See, for example, the meager treatment of the lectionary itself, only a passing mention in nn. 1346 and 1349 of the *Catechism.*

4. *Constitution on the Sacred Liturgy* (December 4, 1963): 24.

5. On the priority of Sunday celebrations in the reform of the Mass, see SC, 49.

6. The so-called postconciliar commission was called the Consilium ("council" in English, which must do for both *consilium* and *concilium* in Latin) for the Implementation of the Constitution on the Liturgy; see Paul VI, motu proprio *Sacram Liturgiam* (January 25, 1964): AAS 56 (1964): 139–44.

7. *The Reform of the Liturgy 1948–1975* (Collegeville, MN: Liturgical Press, 1990): 406–25.

8. See conciliar decree on ecumenism, *Unitatis redintegratio* (November 21, 1964): 6; conciliar pastoral constitution on the Church and the world of today, *Gaudium et spes* (December 7, 1965). On cultural adaptation of the liturgy, see SC, 37–40.

9. See SC, 106, where Sunday is called the *primordialis dies festus.*

10. *Ordo lectionum Missae* (May 25, 1969).

11. COCU, including nine Protestant bodies. For a summary of these and later developments, see "The Story of the Common Lectionary," in *The Revised Common Lectionary,* pp. 75–79.

12. Ronald C. Jasper, liturgical scholar, then a canon of Westminster Abbey, later dean of York Minster. Another observer from the Anglican communion was Massey H. Shepherd, Jr., also a distinguished scholar, professor in the (Episcopalian) Church Divinity School of the Pacific, California.

13. See note 1, above.

14. "Document on the Interpretation of the Bible in the Church," (April 23, 1993). This invaluable study was formally presented by Cardinal Joseph Ratzinger, the commission's president, to John Paul II and warmly welcomed by the latter.

15. "Document on the Interpretation of the Bible in the Church," IV, B.

16. *Praying Together* (Nashville, TN: Abingdon; Norwich, England: Canterbury Press, 1992).

17. Pontifical Council for Promoting Christian Unity, "Directory for the Application of Principles in Ecumenical Matters" (March 25, 1993).

FREDERICK R. MCMANUS

18. "Directory for the Application of Principles in Ecumenical Matters": n. 187.

19. "Document on the Interpretation of the Bible": IV, C, 1.

20. Number 318 of the 1969 *General Instruction of the Roman Missal* makes this option of only two readings available to bishops' conferences "for pastoral reasons." In most countries, including the United States, the three-reading pattern has been faithfully maintained.

page 118   21. SC, 38.

22. Number 45. The omitted sentence acknowledges another development of convergence in liturgical worship: "Some [other ecclesial communities], on the basis of a recommendation expressed at the ecumenical level, have abandoned the custom of celebrating their liturgy of the Lord's Supper only infrequently and have opted for a celebration each Sunday."

Homily
25th Sunday in Anno

GERARD SLOYAN

Reverend Gerard Sloyan preached at the symposium celebrating the twenty-fifth anniversary of the liturgical studies program at Catholic University of America.

>The scripture *readings* for the celebration were:
>
>Amos 8:4 – 7
>
>Psalm 112 (Vulgate):1 – 2, 4 – 6, 7 – 8
>
>1 Timothy 2:1 – 8
>
>Luke 16:1 – 13

It is suggested to readers that they familiarize them*selves* with the biblical texts before reading the homily that follows.

Whoever wrote the first letter to Timothy was someone who wished peace for the late-first-century churches founded or influenced by Saint Paul. The assemblies should pray for figures in authority, that they leave believers in Jesus Christ undisturbed in their tranquil piety. Such prayer is good, and God will be pleased by it, but after this observation, bordering on the banal, there follows what was to prove a theological thunderbolt and then a snatch of hymnody the writer must have sung many times.

The thunderbolt became such only by Saint Augustine's doing. Before that it had been a placid crackling in the summer sky. "God our savior wills every human being to be saved and to come to a knowledge of the truth," the epistle says. The truth is then spelled out in the words of a song: "God is one. So too is the mediator one between God and humanity, the human being Jesus Christ." I render the repeated term *ánthropos* uninfluenced by modern sensibilities. This is the same writer who, a moment later, will limit the public worshipers to men whose hands in every place should be lifted up in prayer, and later still require women's submissive, but not elected, silence in the assembly. In this he let Saint Paul—in whose name he wrote—bear the burden of his prejudice.

Saint Augustine's theory of divine election and reprobation was such, with its conviction that God was ultimately responsible for every human choice, that he could never bring himself to say that God willed all to be saved. He glossed the text. He said it had to mean, "God wills all to be saved who will be saved." Happily the church outvoted him, although you know of the resurgence of his view over the centuries in the West.

But back to First Timothy's snatch of song. They sang about important things in those days: the salvation of all through the mediation of the one who died as a ransom for all. It was best not to show the writer a modern hymn book with its bland assumption on many pages that we pretty much save each other while the one mediator looks complacently on. This horizontal theology with its weak vertical component is a fairly serious matter, not a trivial one, in our worship.

HOMILY

Jesus always knew, as he hung out in bad company and spun his powerful tales, that his Father willed all to be saved. That included the farm managers, crooked as rams' horns, whom Jesus' peasant hearers knew all too well. They were Amos's greedy gougers of the poor, "getting and spending late and soon." But the morality of the characters in Jesus' stories never detained him—their little faults like extortion, torture and occasional slight cases of murder. The conduct of the rich and powerful, as the prophet of Beth-el spelled it out, was utterly reprehensible; but the recital does not fore-shadow Jesus' parable as the lectionary means it to. His story is about something else: "Take a leaf from their book. Watch their methods. See what they do — and do otherwise."

page 121

Our calling, like that of all Christians, is to engage in public praise and thanks to God in ways that befit the divine majesty. We have much to learn from the art forms all about us: the banks that look like shopping malls that look like university student centers; the syncopated rhythms with their unnatural intervals and their unrelenting beat; the talk shows where much is spoken but little is said; the advertising game where everything is new and lit-tle better. This is our culture at its worst, and of it no inculturation is needed.

> The children of this age are shrewder in dealing with
> their own generation than the children of light.
> (Luke 16:8)

If we are enlightened by the light that is Christ, then our path is clear. Upraising our hands to God in public prayer, we must treasure every word that is spoken, choose each one carefully, and waste none of them. The spoken word is precious.

Exorcising the demon of ugliness that surrounds us is our task, putting beauty in its place. The psalms and songs we sing must be melodies of quality and their lyrics high poesy.

GERARD SLOYAN

Sackbut, psaltery and the merry org should resound in our assemblies, but briefly, leaving the hearer longing for more.

Gesture, vesture, clouds of sacred smoke, water and oil and fire, wheaten bread and the fruit of the vine are all to be given tongue with a biblical word.

But will simple folk appreciate any of this, the legendary "Joe six-pack"? Will the young start coming to church in droves? Will the aesthetes deplore the emphasis on prayer and want their sacred concerts back? These questions have their importance, but they are not the great matter. What matters is this: that we give back to the Giver of all good gifts the very best of these gifts, the only Son, in sacrament. We symbolize this exchange by offering to the God of beauty the beauty of the earth. All the world around us is a metaphor for the divine glory. We must let it speak a fitting praise as we engage in this eucharistic, or any sacramental, behavior.